CONTENTS

MY SON

BY PAT KAYE

I have a story to tell. It's about family, love, heartbreak, pain, pride and passion. My son.

On a summer's day he came into my life. It was Wimbledon, strawberries and cream, and Open golf time. Bringing joy, love and pride, that baby of mine. Marcus was his name.

The baby days over, he grew into, at times, a shy child with a love of the outdoors, never happier when on his go-kart and later his bicycle.

Now a boy off to school, off he went with bag in hand and book inside. He loved to read when not riding his bike. Birthday party invites came, but he did not want to go. He'd rather be outdoors.

His love of sports flourished and he joined every team and was no longer shy, but was full of confidence and shone at them all. Golf became his favourite, and everyday he would play to get his handicap down.

Then he found music which became his passion. To the Haçienda he went and his taste changed. He turned his bedroom into a studio with decks and vinyl galore.

His friends would come and make a DIN, which would eventually serve them well. This spilled over to nights at the Angels, doing what he loved making the crowd rave. During the day he played and sold records in many shops in Manchester, and made new friends. His life had changed. Then he found D&B.

HOW YOU MAKE ME FEEL

THE LIFE & LEGACY OF MARCUS INTALEX

BY SHERIF DHAIMISH & MARK O'DONNELL

VELOCITY PRESS

FOR MARCUS AND HIS MUM, PAT.

His reputation grew and the gigs came thick 'n' fast so the day job had to go. He moved to Manchester and shared a house with musicians, all making music and learning their trade, often on trips far away.

Eventually buying his own place with a studio in the loft, he would work on his tunes and when blank he'd stop to eat a pie and then carry on.

Long trips overseas, sometimes with friends, others on his own. On one in New Zealand he met Ayumi. She asked for a track to be played, but he would not. Then sometime later Ayumi was in London. Fate played its hand and they met again. Marcus still wouldn't play the track, but he offered to show her around.

The friendship grew into love and a shared respect. They were happy and had much to look forward to. My child had become a happy man until fate intervened and took him too soon. Many were left in shock. The D&B world came together to share their respects, tributes and awards were made.

Marcus's friends have welcomed me with open arms to their world which he kept me from. They are brothers and sisters who help each other along. A music foundation has been set up to honour his work and nurture up-and-coming musical talent, which Marcus was always happy to do.

The road has been difficult and one I don't want to be on. However, a job needed doing and I did my best with great distress.

KEEP IT CHIPS 'N' GRAVY

If you've visited Burnley on a cold, drizzly day, you might relate to the electronic band KLF's sentiment that 'it's grim up north'. Situated in one of the UK's wettest basins, Burnley sees an average of 216 rainy days annually.

Looming over the town is Pendle Hill, which inspired the local phrase: 'If you can see Pendle, it's going to rain. If you can't see Pendle, it's already raining.' But when the sun emerges and it's crackin' flags, Burnley's cheerful spirit shines through. Rolling hills, vast moorlands and open skies surround the Lancashire town; locals are incredibly proud of their home, even if they've flown the nest.

There's a blunt honesty and wry sense of humour that underpins the town's character. The friends and family of Marcus featured in the early years of this book are the living embodiment of it. And although he relocated to Manchester in the late 90s and travelled the world as a DJ, his hometown remained integral to his identity.

To fans, he was Intalex or Trevino, but to those closest to him in his formative years, he was simply Marcus – straightforward and hard-working. To fully understand Marcus and the man he came to be, you need to take it back to the beginning.

Marcus Julian Kaye was born in Burnley General Hospital on 14 July 1971 and raised by his mother, Pat, a lifelong Burnley FC supporter residing just a stone's throw from Turf Moor stadium – a compact, traditional ground that's been hosting games since 1883. A loving mum with a steadfast spirit, today Pat's home displays keepsakes of Marcus's storied life, including his posthumous Drum&BassArena Hall of Fame award and intricate pencil portraits rendered by his partner Ayumi Maxwell. A framed golf glove, hat, ball and tee also hang in tribute to Marcus's hole-in-one just weeks before his tragic, untimely passing in May 2017.

Following her son's death, Pat started writing. It was a process she found therapeutic. There are two short pieces written by Pat included in this book, one at the beginning and one at the end, where she opens up about her grief, but also the pride she takes in her son's legacy – something she only really became aware of once Marcus was no longer around.

On the morning of Marcus's funeral, his partner Ayumi said to her with a knowing look, 'You're going to be surprised.' Driving towards the crematorium, Pat saw what Ayumi had meant – a sea of people – many in suits, just as many in baseball caps. Marcus's worlds united under Burnley skies to celebrate his life and legacy.

marcusintalex

'The scene of the crime. I struck it sweet, one bounce then out of sight she went. My first ever hole in one, at this yon hole on this yon day Friday 6th May 2017. I have been playing this game on and off for 30 years. Let's hope it dont take that long to get another. I'm off for a pint or two..'

5 May 2017

ROOTS BEFORE BRANCHES

Marcus's childhood was an active one; he was mad about sports. You may have expected Marcus to be musically inclined as a child, glued to his parent's record collection, reading the liner notes and building up his musical knowledge – but that wasn't him. After school Marcus rushed home, then went straight out to play footie with friends, prolonging summer nights until Pat called him home at sundown.

Football has an intensely tribal resonance in Lancashire mill towns like Burnley, Accrington, Blackburn and Preston. Organised league football originally took hold in the late 19th century as an escape for factory workers and labourers. These humble roots grew into a global phenomenon; the English Premier League has become the most watched sports league in the world. Turf Moor stadium represents a hallowed ground for generations of supporters, a source of escapism from the daily grind and a focal point for local pride on matchdays as the town's fortunes ebbed and flowed.

Pat would take Marcus to Burnley home games, a tradition she maintains in his absence to this day. They bonded over their local club, and followed them through thick and thin. There is a lot to be said about following a team like Burnley. Supporting a struggling local football team is one of the ultimate tests of character; your loyalty is pushed to the extreme in the face of consistent disappointment, but you stay true even when it's easier to support bigger clubs with greater riches. Marcus learnt this valuable life lesson early on.

At Towneley High School, he was in the top set class for everything, and showed potential for higher education. Longtime friend Ants Kolaitis recalls how Marcus wasn't necessarily shy, he just 'spoke when he had something to say.' He also worked his way through the ranks in local football teams, including his school's.

ANTS KOLAITIS

At first I didn't like him. I was a right midfielder like him, and he was miles better than me. I was always on the bench waiting for him to play shit, but he didn't.

He was a good player – good at all sports. I remember once we did a competition called STS at school so we could play football in Belgium. We did really well in the competition, but I was never gonna get a game. But because all the lads were together, we'd get a few cans, causing a bit of raucous at night. Nothing serious, just a few Stella. Somehow Marcus ended up injured. There's a picture of the team, and Marcus is in his normal clothes. I took his place and played absolutely shit.

Burnley was once the epicentre of the textile industry, producing more cloth than any other town in Victorian-era Britain and beyond. Its location on the Leeds & Liverpool canal network and wet climate facilitated textile production, powering rapid 19th century growth that drew migrant labourers from surrounding counties and countries including Ireland. However, 20th century deindustrialisation gutted Burnley's coal and cotton economy. The last mines and mills shuttered in the 1980s, leaving economic scars that remain today.

When Marcus came of age in 70s-80s Burnley, the once-thriving industrial hub struggled with job losses in manufacturing and traditional factory work. Social problems emerged, like racial tensions between white British and immigrant South Asian communities, without government support to foster cohesion and integration.

In the midst of this discontent, musical innovation and rebellion was afoot in the region. Punk's raw energy and DIY ethic inspired a generation to form bands or publish fanzines. The north-west had a thriving scene, producing era-defining bands like the Buzzcocks and Joy Division. The influence of electro and hip-hop culture also made its way across the Atlantic. First taking hold in multicultural neighbourhoods like Moss Side and Hulme in Manchester, where Caribbean communities had established a proud tradition of soundsystems, blues parties, pirate radio stations, and dance crews.

The effects of these scenes, with their electrifying creativity and anti-establishment state of mind, rippled outwards, and were felt in towns like Burnley, where they opened the minds and aspirations of their earliest adopters. The *Street Sounds Crucial Electro* compilation series provided the soundtrack.

While some classmates, like Ants, immersed themselves in Burnley's blossoming subcultures – spraying graffiti or breakdancing on flattened cardboard at the town's market – Marcus was still consumed by his love of sport. But by the late 80s, as rave and house began to thrive across East Lancashire's converted warehouses and clubs, there was Marcus spinning records, fully immersed in the scene. His musical journey was about to begin.

Marcus's first love of music was ignited by the sounds of Manchester's legendary Factory Records label. Bands like Durutti Column, Joy Division, New Order, and A Certain Ratio offered new possibilities for a city mired in grim post-industrial depression. Manchester's grey rainy skies, concrete tower blocks, and neglected warehouses provided a stark backdrop. The emerging bands gave a voice to disillusioned young people facing high unemployment and limited prospects.

As New Order subsequently rode the post-punk pathway to global success, Factory Records provided the self-belief that anything was possible in Manchester. The label's Haçienda club was a crucible for the acid house movement in the late 1980s, and became one of the most famous clubs in the world. For Marcus, like many local youths, Factory Records' output in the 80s and the Haçienda defined their coming-of-age.

MARCUS

"I was into everything from Manchester. I bought most of the Factory Records. I had at least one of each of the artists that appeared on Factory.

I was a massive admirer of what Tony Wilson (Factory co-founder) was doing. I really wanted to meet him. I was really struck by what he did for the music of Manchester, the pride he had for the north. He had a weekly TV show... *(So It Goes)*... it was the first time I saw the Stone Roses on there. I went to see them five or six times after that. I saw them at the Haçienda. Just the story of the club, the story of New Order, Joy Division, it led me into other things from Manchester. It got to the point where that's all I listened to for a long time. That's all I needed at the time. It stemmed from my love of synthesised pop music – Depeche Mode. I was a big fan of what Vince Clarke was doing, which kind of led me to New Order. And from *really* being into New Order, I progressed through into early house music and techno."

LATE NIGHT TALES

There comes a pivotal time in teenagers' lives, usually around 15-16 years old, when the temptation of nightlife takes hold. As friends start hanging out in pubs and clubs, having wild escapades that carry on until the birds start tweeting, the prospect of getting up on a Sunday morning and playing football on a muddy pitch loses its appeal. The discipline required to stay in on weekend nights and remain fresh for an early kick-off struggles to compete with the thrill of late nights out. Marcus was no exception to this adolescent rite of passage.

Pat remembers the first time Marcus was caught indulging in Burnley's nightlife after finishing his GCSE exams. This was around the same time he made a trip to the Haçienda to see New Order.

It was the summer of 1987. Marcus went out to play football at 6pm with some friends and he didn't come home until after 1am. I didn't know where he was – but I knew he wasn't playing football.

Marcus had actually met up with some other friends heading to a local nightclub. Worried sick, Pat ended up calling the police. When Marcus finally stumbled in the door, an officer was seated in the living room awaiting his return alongside his frantic mother.

'Where the hell have you been?' I said to him. He was still wearing his shorts and tee with a football under his arm.

Both furious and relieved he was OK, Pat sensed this was the beginning of the end of Marcus coming home at sundown, when the football and goal posts stopped being visible.

DJS TAKE CONTROL

MARCUS

I lived 25 miles north of Manchester in a valley where basically there were no good radio stations. Obviously, 20 years ago (in the 80s) there was no internet, there was no access to anything particularly underground.

I was majorly into a band known as New Order, and I went to see them perform at their own club in Manchester when I was 16 and it was at the Haçienda, which some people might know. To me it's the most influential club of all-time, basically anywhere on the planet. And I saw New Order there and they were pretty good. It wasn't a great gig because you can't see anything. I was a small guy, and there were loads of older people there jumping around.

But the major thing that happened was after New Order finished, a DJ came on. I couldn't even see where the DJ box was – you couldn't see it from where I was stood. I was 16 – this was 1986...87 – it was some time ago. It was the first time I'd been to a club, and the DJ didn't say a word, didn't speak. There was no microphone or nothing, it was just this new music, most of it was sort of early house and little bits of early hip-hop, like Mantronix and things. It was all mixed seamlessly, and I'd never heard anything like it. I was like, 'Oh my God. New Order? Who are they? I want to know more about *this* music.' So basically, I used to travel into Manchester and just go hunting for records.

As Marcus and his classmates stared down the final months of school in 1987, an economic abyss yawned before them, carved open by years of recession under Thatcher's Conservative government. Gloomy job prospects mirrored Burnley FC's disastrous season, narrowly dodging the ignominy of dropping to the lowest league tier by a point.

Marcus committed to Business Studies at Burnley College, lured by the security of accountancy. Pat urged him to continue studying despite the increasing temptation of nightlife, confident that qualifications offered a path towards a stable career, in contrast to the uncertainty they saw around them.

This pragmatic plan quickly unravelled that year following Marcus's first experience at Manchester's legendary Haçienda. It profoundly altered his perspective. He wasn't alone; curious thrill-seekers from struggling surrounding satellite towns were heading to the Haç too, intrigued by its reputation as the place to hear futuristic new sounds and get lost in its hedonistic good times.

Manchester lay 30 miles south of Burnley, requiring a tedious 90-minute bus ride that Marcus began making regularly. To him, Manchester seemed a world apart from Burnley's narrow horizons. In comparison, it was a cultural melting pot where migrant communities from the Caribbean, Ireland, South Asia and beyond made up working-class neighbourhoods like Moss Side, Old Trafford and Cheetham Hill.

Stepping off the bus onto Deansgate, the Victorian architecture and hustle and bustle felt very different to his hometown, but Marcus saw past the imposing facades. Here was a place where things happened, and opportunities were out there. He just needed to find his way somehow.

MARCUS

Coming from Burnley, the only radio I had was BBC Radio 1. I think Jeff Young's show had just started – he was the man before Pete Tong.

I had been introduced to little bits of it but that's it. I think Steve Hurley had been number one with 'Jack Ya Body' (January 1987) out of nowhere. That was the beginning of consciousness for house music for me.

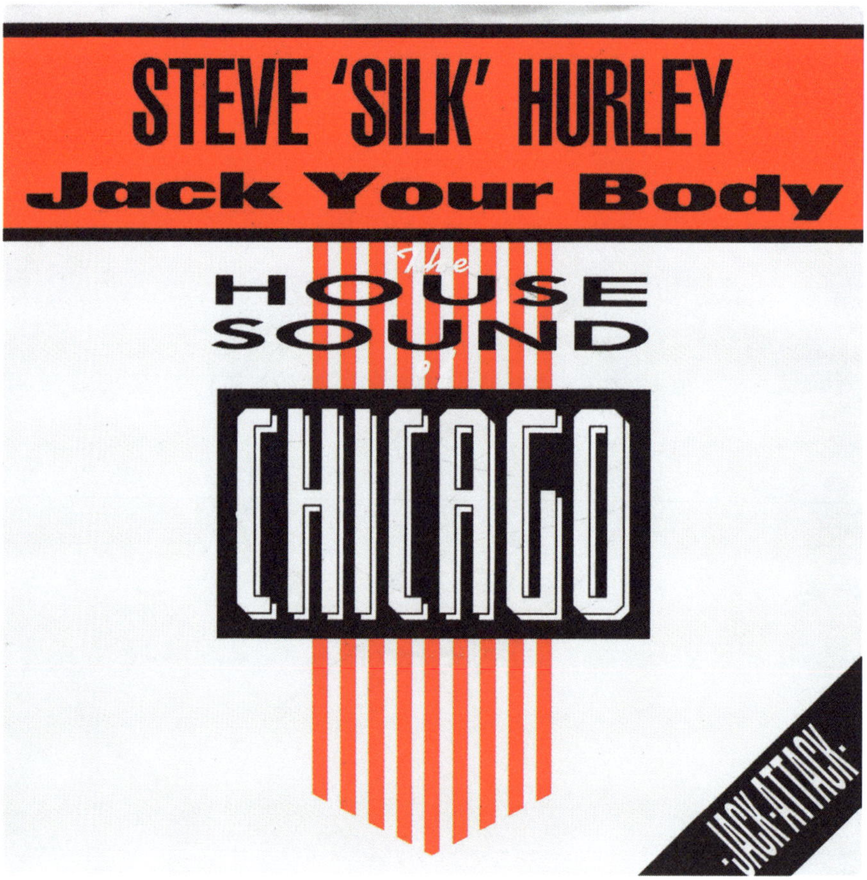

Before going to the Haçienda nightclub for the first time, Marcus had a drink in a nearby bar with some friends. As a 16-year-old who didn't look over 18, he was a bag of nerves.

I had a couple of drinks and felt a bit more ready to get in, but was really worried about not getting in. Walking into a really stylish warehouse, that was instantly a mindblower. I'd never been to a nightclub before and to walk in there was like, *'What the fuck is this?'* (It had) real design behind it. Coming from Burnley I'd never seen anything like it.

The Haçienda opened in 1982, financed by Factory Records as an ambitious yet improbable superclub in a then scrappy artery of the city centre. Initial successes proved elusive, and by 1985 the venue floundered. However, this lull proved to be the calm before the storm as pioneering resident DJs like Mike Pickering began testing nascent sounds from New York, Detroit and Chicago between live sets from bands like New Order.

This bridging of guitar bands and electronic dance music generated a new direction – one serendipitously necessitated by the club's financial woes. Unable to regularly book costly live acts, the Haçienda increasingly turned to extended DJ sets, inadvertently fostering a thriving scene on its dancefloor just as ecstasy was readily available.

When Marcus first attended the Haçienda to see New Order, witnessing the post-show DJ left him utterly transfixed. For the first time he saw the creative possibilities of the DJ role. Just as Chicago house and Detroit techno invented their own distinct 'Midwest' flavour and city identities, the Haçienda developed a uniquely Mancunian vibe. It galvanised the city's independent creatives, many of whom created their own record labels, club nights and clothing brands as a result.

For Marcus and his peers, the Haçienda became a portal to another world. Soon, he'd transition from watching bands on the dancefloor to getting behind the decks at his own events.

A RAVE NEW WORLD

Marcus started working as a glass collector at Smackwater Jack's, a local bar that opened in 1977 as Burnley's answer to the Hard Rock Cafe. By the mid-80s, Smacks, as it was affectionately known, had become a hangout for young locals listening to the latest music from Manchester. His friend Paul Hornsby recalls, 'People tended to gravitate towards each other based on the music they liked and the way they dressed.'

This marked Marcus's introduction to new music, forging friendships over shared interests in their favourite Factory bands and dance tunes. Meanwhile, Marcus struggled to find his footing in college. He confided his dreams of pursuing music to Pat, however improbable they seemed. Like any caring parent, she encouraged him to persist with Business Studies, hoping he would eventually settle into a conventional career. But his mind was elsewhere. In an interview with *Resident Advisor* in 2016, he admitted, 'I wanted to be an accountant, and ended up being a DJ.' The emerging music scene proved too magnetic for him to resist.

PAT KAYE

> **Sometimes you just have to let kids go. I could see that he was content and happy while pursuing music. As a parent, that's a powerful thing.**

Despite lacking experience and the equipment needed, he focused on becoming a DJ. In his mind, it was just a matter of honing his abilities and making the right connections. This demanded ample time and dedication, two resources he had... as well as a set of decks (which he didn't).

MARCUS

“I managed to find a couple of really cool record shops. Every single penny I had, which wasn't much because I was 16 and had a newspaper round which is like £10 a week, I spent that on records.

It was basically the love of early house music and the movement. It was more so the movement than the music to an extent. It was this crazy, exciting thing that hadn't existed before. I was getting into something that nobody knew anything about, and we were all growing up together, and really getting into this music...”

Marcus was well-positioned at Smacks to get access to the latest parties and happenings in the local area. Outside of licensed clubs, the rave and free party scene was spreading like wildfire in the late 80s. For many, this was a counter-culture movement sticking two fingers up at a government that had turned its back on Britain's working class and entire regions facing drastic decline. To others, it was one big party that they never wanted to end.

Despite the economic uncertainty, Marcus had a bit of money from his part-time jobs, most of which would be pumped back into vinyl, equipment and clothes. This shift from being a football-obsessed teen to immersing himself in the rapidly evolving underground scene came out of nowhere for his former schoolmate, Ants.

ANTS KOLAITIS

He was never into electro or breakdancing. When me and my mates got into the house scene, it was a natural progression for us.

Marcus was playing for some decent teams in football. I hadn't seen him for about 18 months during that period. But then the Bank Hall Miners night came up. I saw Marcus and he'd grown his hair longer – it was a bit greasy. I was surprised. 'What are you doing here? How come you're into this?' Little did I know he was already well into the music.

Marcus's hometown Burnley and nearby towns like Blackburn were instrumental in the movement. Often collectively referred to as the 'Blackburn Raves', these DIY parties became a big part of Marcus and his friends' lives. In between his trips to Manchester, they would head to raves in the local area, giving them an opportunity to hear the music they were picking up from Manchester's record shops. Folk would meet at Smackwater Jack's where they'd find out what was going on, and then move on from there to party into the wee small hours.

With an orbit of disused warehouses dotted around the region, ravers were recycling space that was once occupied by their predecessors, grafting to the relentless beat of the looms. Makeshift parties began springing up all over the place.

The night at the Bank Hall Miners that Ants refers to took place in May 1988, and proved to be a seminal night, not just for Marcus, but others involved. The venue was originally a northern soul venue.

FREEZER
A CASE OF SERIOUS COLD CHILLIN!
House
TODD TERRY
Techno
DELA
New Beats!
UNAME IT
ICE WET TO BE COOL
BUZZ B.
Hip/House
808 STATE
COOL POOL
THIS SURE BEAT'S WORKIN FOR ME!
Deep
45 King
Acid
Rap
Mr Fingers
101 D.J.s
DRESS TO SWEAT!
THIS IS YOUR UPFRONT MUSIC 'SCENE'.
QUALITY SOUNDS, NO POP CHARTS!
SO COME ON BROTHERS AND SISTERS!
SET IT OFF!
BANK HALL MINERS FRIDAY MAY 5th
8p.m.–late. £1 before 10p.m., £1·50 after.

House Rave: Saturday 9.30 to 2.00
TONYS
All night Partys to follow!
LEGAL LEGAL LEGAL LEGAL LEGAL
LEGAL
ROCKIN
D.J. — where's the BASS?
Party People
Blackburn Town Centre
BASS
Gilly & Marcos with Celebrity D.J.'s
Top One What?

MARCUS

We started to do parties in our town which is just the smallest, dumbest provincial town in England.

People used to go out, get drunk, have a kebab, have a fight, if you're lucky you got a girl. That was just the brains and mentality of it. But from one week to the next you'd see 10 people, 20 people, two months later 200 people. There's another town down the road, a place called Blackburn which is notorious if you come from Burnley. It's about 20 miles away – not even that, probably ten, and because of the football, nobody from Burnley could be seen in Blackburn or you'd get beat up, except for when this music started. And when this music started, we could go to Blackburn, and the people who wanted to beat you up now wanted to kiss you, say hello, chat to you, grab and hold you and stuff ... Obviously some drugs were involved in this, but it completely changed the mentality of everybody, and so this is what makes it exciting. Just being involved in this thing changed your entire thought process.

These were the first pulses of acid house in Lancashire. It created a place where tribal barriers between football rivals and different towns temporarily disappeared. As Lancashire continued to grapple with the effects of deindustrialisation, many got involved in the rave scene and created something new in the remnants. Like Manchester, and even as far away as Berlin and Detroit, where factories lay empty but musical passions burned, Burnley's in-the-know youth rallied around the DIY rave community rather than abandon hope or escape toward London's brighter lights.

Perhaps something in this cultural defiance resonated for Marcus too, as he pivoted from the pitch to the dancefloor, realising that change was stirring locally. The makeshift raves suited Burnley's spirit. Marcus jumped headfirst into the scene, his world and the possibilities within it expanding to the beat of the drum.

Tony's
Blackburn
Right in the centre of town.
Next to the Pizza Hut, Across from the Library
Open Saturdays 10-2.am
THE ORB
DJs GILLY + MARCUS
HOUSE MUSIC ALL NIGHT
TONYS NEW EMPRES
BALLROOM
TOWN HALL ST. BLACKBUR

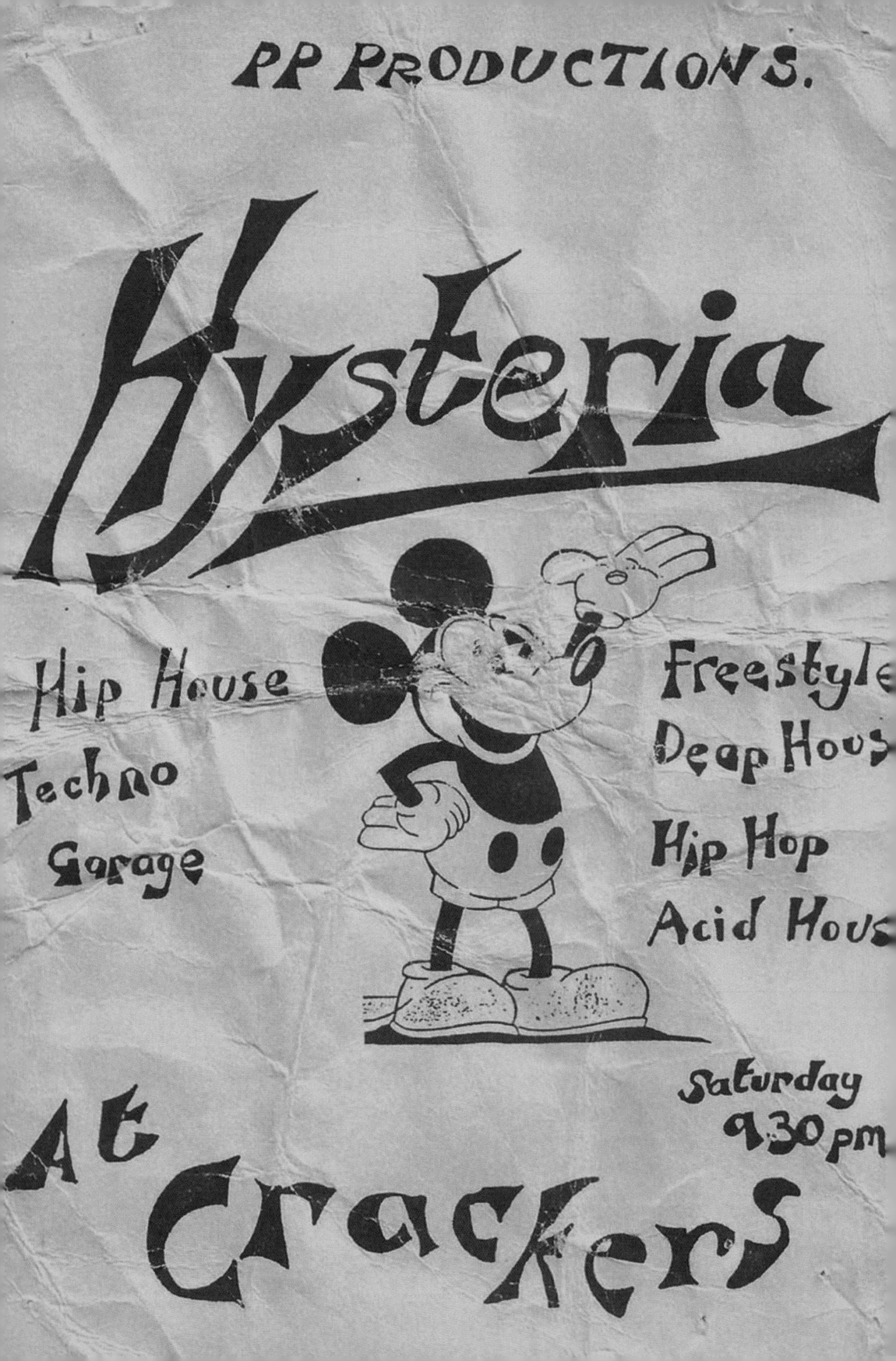
PP PRODUCTIONS.
Hysteria
Hip House
Techno
Garage
Freestyle
Deep Hous
Hip Hop
Acid Hous
Saturday
9.30 pm
At
Crackers

A NEW DIRECTION
PRESENTS

euphoria (PART I)

THE KESTREL SUITE
(BURNLEY) FRI 1st SEPT
9-00Pm TILL LATE
CONSISTING OF
3 TOP DJ.s
MIXING, CUTTING, SCRATCHING
FULL VISUAL'S
BE EARLY – DRESS TO 'RAVE'
admission only (£2·50)
techno / house/hip hop/garage / free style / world beats

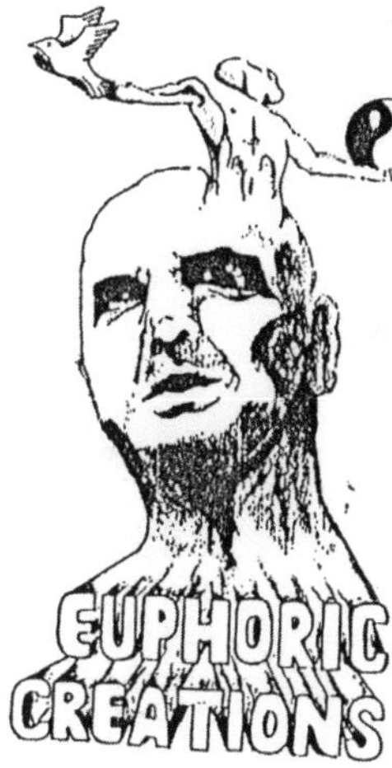

CHILL~OUT

AT
THE **HOP**
EVERY SUNDAY
NITE
7:30 TILL 10:30
TRAFALGAR ST
BURNLEY

D.J.'s
GILLY (TONYS)
MARCUS (ANGELS, MUNROES)

CHEAP DRINKS ALL NITE
50p IN AFTER 9:00pm
MANAGEMENT RESERVE THE RIGHT
TO REFUSE ADMISSION

T TUNES
O SYSTEM
P BUZZ

300 hel
acid s

By RALPH MARSHALL

POLICE in riot gear were bombarded with fireworks, wooden staves and metal as they fought to break up an illegal acid house party.

Nearly 300 revellers were arrested after barricading themselves in as officers battered down a door and came under attack early yesterday.

Revellers' attack on police

Today the deputy chairman of Lancashire police committee, Coun Eric Allcock, said he would be asking the chief constable the reasons for the scale of arrests.

Truncheon-wielding police with dogs scattered party-goers at Brownside Mill, Worsthorne, Burnley, and lined them against the walls of the 5,000 sq ft empty unit as a fleet of police vans came to take them to nine East Lancashire police stations.

A total of 284 young people were arrested, a few for assault and the rest for public order offences.

They were later released on police bail or reported. Burnley Supt Clive Fothergill said a quantity of drugs were found on the premises.

He said no officers were injured in the operation, involving police from throughout the county. One party-goer was treated for a minor injury after being burned on the leg by a firework.

The industrial unit at Brownside Mill, Worsthorne.

■ P

l in
oop

e' cars outside the mill.

Neighbours in nearby Brun Terrace said they alerted police after being awakened by dozens of cars pulling up outside their homes shortly before 3am.

Word that the former Barker May joinery works was to be the venue for Burnley's first acid house party was relayed in Burnley, Accrington and Blackburn clubs and at M62 service points late on Saturday. Many young people came from Leeds and Manchester.

They paid £5-a-head to attend the party after the unit had been broken into, but police arrived in force shortly after 5am.

Huddled

One Burnley girl who attended, a stock controller who wanted only to be named as Donna, said several people were hit by truncheons and police shields as officers swarmed into the unit, smashing up the sound equipment.

"We were all huddled in a corner and the police lined us up against the walls of the unit until the vans arrived," she added.

One girl claimed she had been strip-searched in police cells and other revellers said their cars had been damaged or immobilised by officers.

Police say party-goers caused around £1,200 damage to the unit which is owned by a Huddersfield development company.

Coun Allcock said: "It does seem a lot of arrests and more than at other parties but I have every confidence in the judgment of the police."

LANCASHIRE EVENING TELEGRAPH MONDAY NOVEMBER 26 1990

A WAY OF LIFE

JASON FROST

"We all grew up through the Factory Records era, New Order and so on. That led us to the Record Peddler at the end of Oldham Street, which would sell the old Factory Records and stuff.

And that led us to the Haçienda around 1987, and onto Eastern Bloc (a well-known record shop) when it was in Affleck's Palace. Martin from 808 State used to work there. I was working in a factory for £70 a week, and Marcus was at college. About £40 of that would go on records. We'd go into Eastern Bloc, and we got to know Martin. He'd bring up the latest Chicago and Detroit house for us and I'd buy it. They'd all somehow end up at Marcus's house...

In 1988, Marcus, me and two of our friends Balko and Taj went to London to look for acid house. We went to the Wag Club in Soho and the Fridge in Brixton. We wanted to go to Heaven, which was Oakenfold's night, but we didn't. We came back and set up a night in Burnley, which Balko ran. It was at the Thompson Centre, the local sports centre in Burnley. Me, Marcus, Taj and Balko were DJing there. We'd get about 100 people through the door which was mental. We would walk down the street in our smiley t-shirts, Converse on, all that kind of stuff. People would shout 'Acieeed' to us as we walked down the street, like in that tune by D-Mob. Four or five weeks into the night, some-one smashed the toilets up and we got kicked out.

So from there, we went to places like Angels. We were into the Manchester baggy thing and a bit of house music, and that was it. Some weeks we'd get in, some weeks we wouldn't because we looked a bit scruffy. Paul Taylor was the main man there. He was a big influence on me and Marcus when we first started going out.

He was playing Gil Scott-Heron 'The Bottle', and jazz-funk. There's people like Kenny O'Shea and Ady Hurst who were a big influence on us too. They were the cool kids in baggy pants; we used to call them the 'Accy Dancers', as in people from Accrington.

At that point, Taylor was playing house music, but it was like the acid (house) remix of Wee Papa Girl Rappers. It wasn't really stuff we were listening to. Now I remember Marcus going up to Alan Durkin who owned the place and saying, 'This is shit.' Durkin said, 'You think you can do better, do you?' 'Fuckin' right I do,' Marcus said. Durkin said he'd give us a Tuesday night. We came out and thought, 'Fuckin' hell! We've got a Tuesday night at Angels.' The day after, the scale of it dawned on us. We weren't on that level at all. Marcus said, 'What are we gonna do? We haven't even got any decks.' So he had the gall to call Alan Durkin and say, 'Listen mate, you couldn't lend us some decks, could you?' And just like that, Durkin gave us some decks. They were in a suitcase.

There'd always be this little argument with me and Marcus about who'd nicked whose records. I'd buy all the records at Eastern Bloc, and he'd have the suitcase decks. He would be skiving from college learning to mix at home. I remember when I went round in the evenings, Pat used to bang on the ceiling with a brush and tell us, 'That's ENOUGH!' ”

Marcus's first time DJing to an audience was in spring 1988 at the Thompson Centre, Burnley's local leisure centre, home to swimming and diving pools, roller discos, and basketball courts. Despite being short-lived and only lasting for a few weeks, Marcus and friends grew an organic following of young partygoers and crafted a setting to immerse in the new, rapidly evolving music. Clubs in the area were catching on to the music, but homegrown raves and parties were at the heart of the movement, which is lovingly documented in the book *Flashback: Parties for the People by the People* (Rough Trade, 2021) – a firsthand account of what was going on in the area at the time.

Described as a 'post-industrial quagmire' by DJ and friend of Marcus, Bodie Cameron, music and parties offered an exhilarating escape from the mundane. Friendships and networks were formed, and Marcus was beginning to meet people who shared his love for the music and scene. This included Nigel Gilmartin, known locally as Gilly.

A few years Marcus's senior, Gilly was a master at finding venues for local nights and was pivotal in east Lancashire's rave movement. He was like the Pied Piper, rocking up at Smacks with a mixtape for Marcus to play, and rounding up people in minibuses to go to parties. Gilly was responsible for setting up some of the most legendary nights in the area, whether in warehouses, clubs or function rooms, and driving house music forward. He would transform local pubs and spaces into a raver's paradise. In places like the Tavern in Great Harwood, he would set up decks, a smoke machine and lights while regulars were coming in for a pint, having no clue what was going on as young people in baggy t-shirts danced the night away.

Recognising Marcus's talent early on, Gilly had him DJ at various events he promoted. Hand-drawn flyers from these parties featured Marcus and Gilly's names side-by-side. During this period the two names became synonymous with each other.

GILLY

"**The first time I met Marcus, Jack and Ants, I was putting up flyers in Burnley town centre for a night I was putting on in May 1988 with Mr Freeze at the Bank Hall Miners.**

I had my Converse on, Kangol hat on and was just sticking flyers up around Burnley, which wasn't my area. I'm from Accrington. I tended to put them up around bus stops. You had to be brazen. I remember them coming up to me later on while I was on stage: 'Can we come up and look at your records?' We realised we were into the same stuff.

It all went off from that night, really. I started coming over to Smacks in Burnley, and I'd bring a tape with me to see if Marcus would put it on while he was working. Me and Marcus started DJing together at places like the Kestrel Suite in Burnley, but we had to pack it in because all the Burnley lads were threatening us. It got sorted in the end, but the football hooliganism thing was massive then.

Back at an after party in Nelson that night, I asked Marcus if he wanted to come and join us and DJ at Monroe's in Great Harwood, and that took things to another level."

MARCUS

"Basically everyone gave up what they were doing to go raving. Even going to the bar for a few drinks, that stopped. The weekend went on longer. In fact, the weekend never stopped for some people.

It brought drugs right into the limelight, probably (for the first time) since the 1960s. It was just so exciting. I think half of it was the illegal side of it – people breaking into warehouses. Probably the most exciting part of it for me was actually trying to find the venues and just being with these thousands of people trying to do the same thing. Police trying to cordon us off, putting roadblocks up. Sometimes there were fights with the police and guards getting turned over. I'm not condoning that but just to witness it all, it completely changed my life forever.

As well as the music, it was the way of life. They are grey places – they are grim. Entertainment is massive there. The less money there is, the less sunshine, the less beaches there are to go to, people still want a release and they find it through different things. I think that's why UK music is a great place because it is a bit grey and grim."

KEEP OUT!

Burnley on acid house drug party alert

POWER
HOUSE
THE ATMOSPHERE IS BACK
MONROES
GREAT HARWOOD, Nr. BLACKBURN
TOP MIXERS
JOHN J
MARCUS
plus Guest DJ's
FRIDAYS 9.30 - 2.00
SATURDAYS 9.00 - 2.00
No.1 WEEKEND VENUE

The emergence of DIY parties in the area provided a training ground for Marcus's early forays as a DJ. Music had swiftly become a way of life. He would even regularly travel to towns like Ramsbottom, closer to Manchester than Burnley, to pick up the Sunset 102 FM signal and listen to DJs Mark XTC (Mix Factory) and 808 State/Spinmasters. Inspired by what he was absorbing on the airwaves and at parties, he was quickly making a name for himself at Monroe's in Great Harwood, one of the clubs Gilly had helped get off the ground.

Monroe's was formerly known as Cloggers, a social club that occasionally had DJs playing the latest hits, and was a popular nightspot in the area. Gilly was originally invited to become the resident DJ around 1986 and was expected to play chart music. However, his collection was starting to include cultured disco cuts like 'Jingo' by Candido and Hamilton Bohannon records, and he was also picking up early house records like Farley 'Jackmaster' Funk's 'Love Can't Turn Around' and Steve 'Silk' Hurley's 'Jack Your Body'. The crowd loved it, but the owners didn't. He eventually got fired because he refused to play chart cheese.

This led him to explore smaller venues, such as the Tavern pub and the Kestrel Suite in Burnley. He co-promoted these events with Marcus, where they could freely play house music. When Gilly was asked to return to Monroe's by new owners, he brought Marcus along for the ride. The new management had seen the popularity of house music go through the roof and wanted a piece of the action.

Monroe's was quickly established as one of the best places in the area to listen to underground music on a Thursday night, which soon became Fridays and Saturdays, due to demand. Alongside residents like Gilly and Marcus, leading Manchester act the Jam MCs would visit.

Gilly recalls how Marcus was a pure natural talent on the decks, and guest DJs would recognise this too.

GILLY

Other DJs at Monroe's were well into Marcus's style, the sort of chop mixing he did, which was inspired by the Jam MCs – they were the pioneers of that.

They would have two tracks, with the crossfader switching from one to the other, fusing two records together while they were playing. Marcus just took to it without even practising. It was bizarre how he was almost telepathic with it. That's how gifted he was in that department. He just had something totally different that no one else had.

Marcus's raw talent and adventurous style of DJing was beginning to carry weight locally. Neil Jackson, who was DJing in the area at the same time as Marcus, remembers some of the tricks he was able to pull off while performing on what would today be considered pretty basic equipment.

NEIL JACKSON

I first heard Marcus DJ at the Kestrel Suite in the 80s. He dropped 'Airport '89' by Wood Allen – it's a bit cheesy now but I still love it.

I'd heard of Marcus being on at Monroe's. He was well into the technicality of it all. I remember hearing he'd do these effects with the decks, like a deck stop or a spin back. He would also put the top of an aerosol can over the top of the spindle, put a record on top of that so there's a four-inch gap between the platter and the record. He'd centralise it as much as possible, then put a weight on top of it to keep it in place.

Then he'd get the headshell, which has a pin at either side that slots into the tone arm of the Technics 1210, and it screws on. If you take that off and turn it upside down and the needle's facing upwards, you can turn it on and it still works. Then you take the weight off the back so it flips it up, and then you put the record on the underside of the needle and it plays the record backwards. So Marcus was doing that at Monroe's, playing all this weird shit out.

This sample playlist of a Marcus set at Monroe's showcases what was heating up the scene at the time: energetic dancefloor grooves, uplifting piano house, and the odd early Belgian banger so it wasn't too 'happy'. Italo house would soon begin to dominate a lot of the club scene, something Marcus wasn't on board with, and which can be sensed from his setlists just a year later.

MARCUS KAYE'S SETLIST

MONROE'S 1990

11. Octave One – *I Believe*
12. Mysterious – *Electro Shock*
13. 2 In A Room – *Wiggle It (As it Grooves)*
14. Lee Marrow – *Movin'*
15. Catch – *Free*
16. House Crew – *Dance to the House (Strictly)*
17. Radical Rob – *Monkey Wah*
18. Kamera – *Back In the Time*
19. Earth People – *Dance (Dub Mix)*
20. Cee Jay – *Confession*
21. Shamen – *Progen (Land of Oz)*
22. Don Pablos Animals – *A Different Story*
23. Casa Nostra – *Insomnia*
24. Julie Wright – *Its Alright With Me*
25. Pret A Porter – *Mystere De L'Amour*
26. Pierre Feroldi – *Movin Now*
27. Manic MCs – *The Beat*
28. Trak One – *Motion*
29. Wendel Williams – *Everybody*
30. 24 Seven – *I Cant Stand It (Bruce Forrest Remix)*
31. Neon – *Dont Mess With This Beat*
32. Reese – *Rock to the Beat (Hitman Mix)*
33. 808 State – *Cubik (Remix)* & Yello – *Unbelievable Live Mashup*
34. D-Shake – *Techno Trance*
35. Seduction – *One Mistake* & Nicole – *Rock the House*

Monroe's is still remembered as one of the area's most unpretentious and raw nightclubs; it provided ravers a home for well over a decade. Marcus was a part of its evolution and helped bring in crowds from across the country who were in search of the freshest underground sounds. It was also a place where people – at least temporarily – set aside turf wars.

GILLY

“ **In the early days of Monroe's with me and Marcus on, he brought loads of people from Burnley.**

I had a lot of respect in my town – Great Harwood and Blackburn – so when locals were kicking off with people from out of town I'd get in the middle of it and say, 'Listen, this is a new fuckin' thing. It's not like what it was when it was Cloggers. This is different, a new regime about house music and people coming together.' Football and all them rivalries were out of the window. It worked, everyone started becoming mates. It was a game-changer. ”

Even so, old rivalries die hard. And it wasn't all peace and love on the dancefloor. Burnley and Blackburn's two teams – Burnley FC and Blackburn Rovers – have a hatred for one another that runs as deep as any football rivalry goes. Accrington Stanley sit in the middle of the two clubs, yet neither one considers them a serious rival or enemy. At the time Marcus was beginning to DJ the clubs' supporters had been at each other's throats for a hundred years. 'Bastard Rovers!' and 'Burnley Bastards!' are some of the friendlier terms the opposing teams use towards each other.

Marcus and Gilly's friendship was a small but significant step towards unifying people. The music scene grew into a coalescing force. The availability of ecstasy allowed barriers to be broken down, creating a collective sense of euphoria and empathy. It was a fleeting, band-aid solution perhaps, but a positive one, nonetheless.

MARCUS

They started taking ecstasy and there was a completely different feeling. People wanted to talk to each other, and celebrate the scene.

Celebrate the fact they were doing something brand new and exciting. Even though there was still the rivalry there it didn't matter whatsoever. In fact, I remember there was one guy we all knew who had a reputation for using knives when it was the football fighting.

A guy from Burnley who got knifed by him was in the same club as him, and they started talking to each other. That would have never happened three years previous. That's a real extreme, but it did change that aspect of clubbing.

blindfaith
DO YOU BELIEVE?
HERE MARCUS +
GILLY PREACH
EVERY FORTNIGHT
STARTS MAY 12th
KESTEREL SUITE
BURNLEY: SUNDAYS
COMMENCES 7PM
£2: ADMITS ONE
LIMITED NUMBERS
ART BY ICARUS
THE POWER OF THE RAVE
THE LIGHT IGNITES

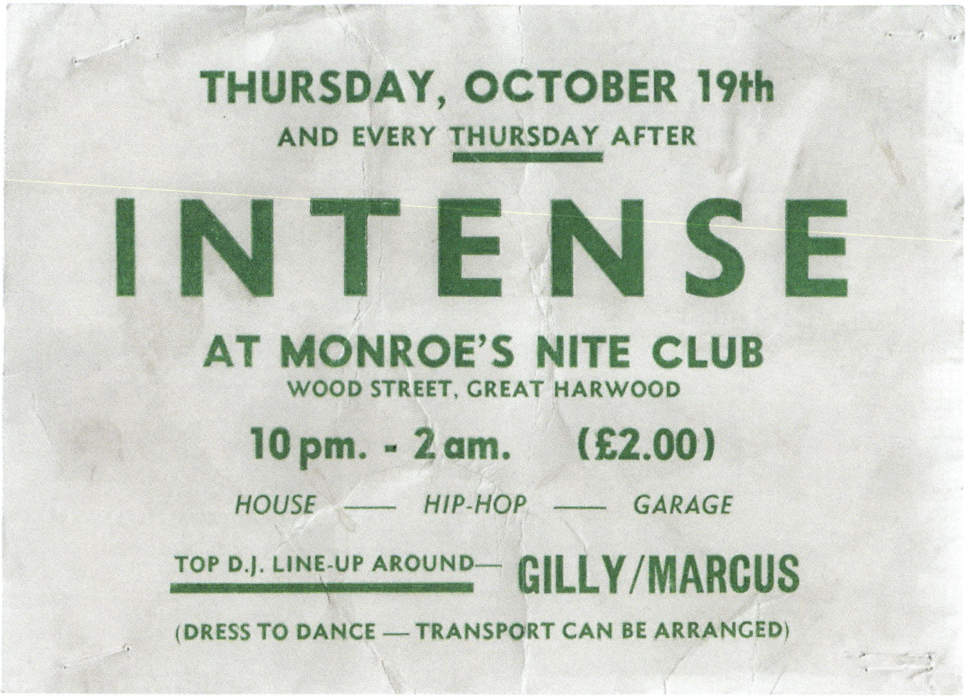
THURSDAY, OCTOBER 19th
AND EVERY THURSDAY AFTER
INTENSE
AT MONROE'S NITE CLUB
WOOD STREET, GREAT HARWOOD
10 pm. - 2 am. (£2.00)
HOUSE —— HIP-HOP —— GARAGE
TOP D.J. LINE-UP AROUND— GILLY/MARCUS
(DRESS TO DANCE — TRANSPORT CAN BE ARRANGED)

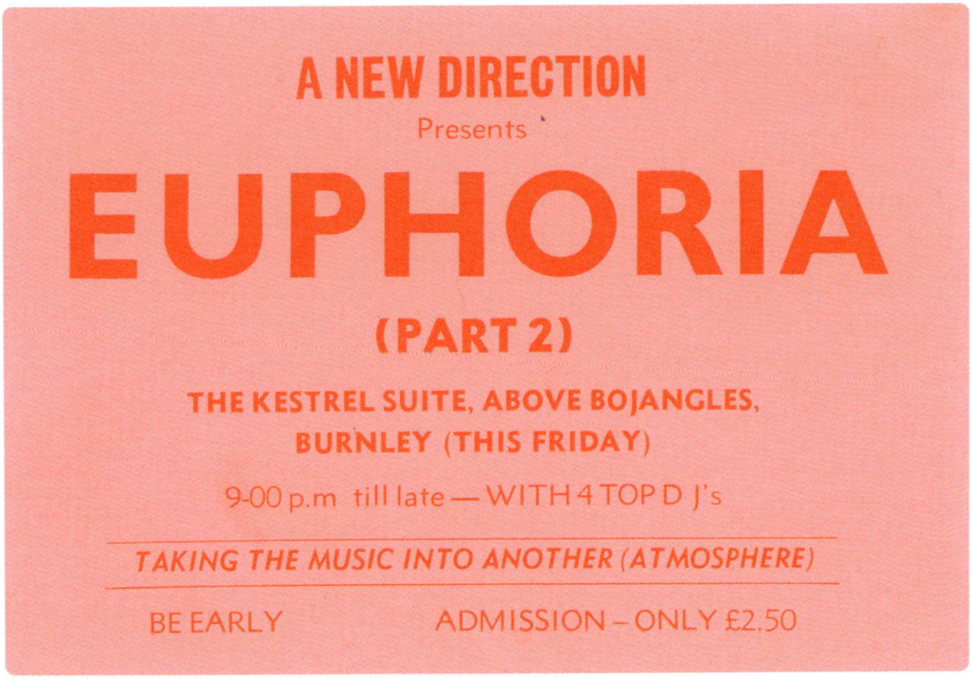
A NEW DIRECTION
Presents
EUPHORIA
(PART 2)
THE KESTREL SUITE, ABOVE BOJANGLES,
BURNLEY (THIS FRIDAY)
9-00 p.m till late — WITH 4 TOP D J's
TAKING THE MUSIC INTO ANOTHER (ATMOSPHERE)
BE EARLY
ADMISSION – ONLY £2.50

EXPRESS YOURSELF

The emergence of rave culture and mass underground dance events sparked intense public anxiety in the region and across the UK. Police and politicians, stirred up by newspaper headlines depicting it as a corrupting and dangerous influence, ultimately came up with the draconian Criminal Justice and Public Order Act 1994 (c. 33), which introduced a number of changes to the law, most notably clamping down on unlicensed rave parties, and giving greater powers to the police to confiscate equipment and prosecute the organisers.

Newspapers and broadcasters increasingly sensationalised the recreational drug use, illegal warehouse parties, and perceived recklessness associated with raves. There were numerous scare stories about depraved behaviour and connections to crime syndicates. This social panic characterised ravegoers, especially working-class youth, as feral, criminal, and vulnerable to moral corruption. This rave in Padiham, a neighbouring town to Burnley, is a prime example of the local media's perception of what was happening.

AFTERMATH OF AN ACID HOUSE PARTY

***Burnley Express*, 13 February 1990, Altham Industrial Estate, Padiham**

Trail of damage as 5,000 dance through the night at industrial estate. The latest craze in acid house parties came to the Burnley area in the early hours of Sunday. More than 5,000 revellers left a trail of tin cans and litter in their wake after a nine hour party in an empty unit on the Altham Industrial Estate just outside Padiham. Police arrested 25 people for alleged drug related offences following the party. It is believed drug dealers could have been selling drugs in two small offices in the unit. As the party got going a neighbouring unit containing wall coverings was broken into and £25 cash, chocolate bars and biscuits stolen and fire extinguishers let off. At least one car was broken into and a cassette radio stolen while the empty unit and surrounding car park and yard were strewn with litter. It was shortly after 1 am that a cortege of cars, many of them thought to be from the Blackburn area, started to arrive on the industrial estate. Admission was £5 with party-goers queuing outside to get in and dance to the latest house music. During the night people were dancing on the roofs of smaller office units within the warehouse which has been empty for about six months. Police say they had an adequate presence on the estate. There were no arrests for public order offences and police prevented serious damage to other premises.

Despite this – or perhaps as an unintended result of the extensive press coverage – the scene continued to spread, with some organisers becoming increasingly inventive about where they hosted parties and other promoters moving into licensed clubs and venues. Where there was house/rave music, there were people ready to drop whatever they were doing to party. Marcus had already displayed a steely commitment to the cause – and his profile as a DJ was on the rise. This wasn't just a phase; it was a path where doors were opening all the time. Crucially, it was an environment he felt at home in, and was able to freely express himself.

GRAHAM 'GRUMPY' NAYLOR

"There were loads of warehouse parties all over the north-west. People were tipping up from all over the country. It's all a bit of a blur now, but when you've got cockneys on your doorstep, you know something special is happening. These were great times!

One of my most memorable Marcus gigs was at a 'nightclub' in Bradford. It was literally in the middle of a terraced street. Someone had gutted the place, knocked through the downstairs. It had a DJ booth at the far end of the room and some big booming speakers. The door to the right of the DJ booth went upstairs to a plush bar, chrome and mirrors everywhere.

It was like the James Bond film, *Octopussy*. One minute you're raggamuffin it, sat on a sofa in a scruffy bar, then it revolves around into the bling of a villain's lair. I'm not saying whoever had converted that part of the street into a nightclub was up to anything dodgy, but..."

ANGELS OF THE NORTH-WEST

Burnley's Angels nightclub was a well-known spot on the UK club scene, as disco morphed into early house and the rave years. Open since the mid-70s, Angels' transformation flowed with the shifting tides in the underground scene. Run by Scottish DJ/producer Paul Taylor, the club punched way above its weight for a venue in a relatively small town until its closure in 1996. In the 70s, it gave northern soul and disco a home; in the late 80s Taylor reinvented Angels for ravers. UK pioneers like Shut Up & Dance, DJ Hype, Carl Cox and Sasha featured; even former boxing world champion Nigel Benn DJed there.

For many ravers from this era, Marcus remains synonymous with Angels rather than his later achievements in jungle, drum & bass and techno. This was a special time for those who got to see him regularly. His Friday night Vision residency started in 1990 and gave him the confidence to know he could rock the dancefloor as much as the big-name guests, some of who became future friends and collaborators (notably Doc Scott and Mark XTC).

One night in the early 90s, as the club pulsated to the low-end bass pumping out of the PA, a young DRS first got on the mic for Marcus. He wasn't a 'raver', as hip-hop was his first love, but he could see how the music lent itself to a live MC, and asked Marcus if he could have a go on the mic despite having no club experience. DRS's freestyling thrilled the crowd and prompted Marcus to encourage him to do more of it, planting the seed for their creative partnership in years to come.

Angels was a more professionally run club than Monroe's, as it was essentially a discotheque-turned-rave cave. It had a bigger capacity which it would often exceed to accommodate those who had travelled from across the UK; the sound system was huge, and it had a dazzling array of lasers and lights.

MARCUS

"I started the Friday nights in Angels. It went from having nobody in to having coachloads arrive from Scotland, and all across the UK. It was a sell-out – the capacity was 600 but we'd have 1,100 in there every Friday for like two or three years."

BODIE CAMERON

"I met Marcus whilst working at Angels in 1990. I'd just been given the Friday warm-up slot for the Vision nights and Marcus had become resident after tearing the roof off on Tuesdays there, in and around Burnley, and at Monroe's in Great Harwood.

On one particular Friday I found a box in the booth before opening time; it was Marcus's and I couldn't help playing a couple out of it (thinking no one was around). He asked me later if I had played out of his box and I 'fessed up. He was very relaxed about it. Later that night he pulled a copy of Landlord 'I Like It' and Bonesbreaks 'Janet's Revenge' out of my box and proceeded to create in a way I'd never seen a DJ create. So much precision, so much style. Such a lesson learnt! To this day I'm sure this pre-dated Carl Cox's 'Let The Bass Kick' mashup (a track that combined both of the tracks mentioned above).

It was a very brief but important time in the history and development of music for us all. Burnley was a post-industrial quagmire, and all many of us had was this new sound and culture. A-list DJs and artists from all over the country would come and play here. Marcus always held his own and more often than not surpassed them. For myself and many, many people, he is an inspiration. A council estate kid that took what that small town, club and time had taught us around the world, and always remained authentic, stylish and humble."

DJ HYPE

"The first time I met Marcus Intalex was in a club called Angels in Burnley, his hometown, in about 1992... how time flies."

Kiss FM Marcus Intalex tribute mix - 31 May 2017

GRAHAM 'GRUMPY' NAYLOR

> **"Me and Marcus both loved early DJ Hype stuff. Marcus taped a Fantasy FM set of his – I'm guessing around 1990. One of the tracks on it was 'Radio Babylon' by Meat Beat Manifesto – Choooooon! It must've been copied by half of Burnley – this was the shit."**

Marcus cultivated a dedicated following for his sets which featured the latest techno and emerging UK breakbeat hardcore. This set him apart from Taylor's vocal piano house style that dominated Saturday nights at Angels. Over the course of a year or two, Marcus was drawing heavily from forward-thinking labels like R&S, Underground Resistance, XL, Suburban Base and Reinforced, reflected in jaw-twisting tracks like the playlist below.

VISION PLAYLIST

TRACKS 9-20 SELECTED BY BODIE CAMERON

01. Joey Beltram – *My Sound*
02. M.N.O. – *God of Abraham*
03. Meat Beat Manifesto – *Radio Babylon*
04. X-ES – *Do You Wanna Dance*
05. Channel X – *Rave the Rhythm*
06. The Prodigy – *Everybody in the Place*
07. Cubic 22 – *Night in Motion*
08. M&M – *Don't Stand in my Way*
09. Reese and Santonio – *Rock to the Beat*
10. Underground Resistance – *Amazon*
11. Rhythm is Rhythm – *Nude Photo*
12. Bobby Konders – *Nervous Acid*
13. Paperclip People – *Oscillator*
14. Orange Lemon – *Dreams of Santa Anna*
15. 4hero – *Mr. Kirk's Nightmare*
16. Genaside II – *Narra Mine*
17. G Double E – *Fire When Ready*
18. Smart Systems – *Tingler*
19. Underkut – *Both Ends*
20. Carl Cox – *Let the Bass Kick*

PARADISE
PARADISE

DJ GREENBINS

Every time I hear Renegade Soundwave's 'Space Gladiator' – and I mean EVERY TIME – I think of Marcus Intalex! We did a back-to-back at Angels in Burnley on a Friday night when he was known as Marcus Kaye. We dropped this over and over all night.

Like the very best resident DJs, he knew exactly how to work the crowd, when to take listeners on a musical journey, and when to unleash absolute pandemonium on the dancefloor. The club would remain a spiritual home for Marcus, right up until its closure in 1996, despite his appearances becoming more sporadic in the latter years. He met a lot of allies in music there, and although his increased preference for darker breakbeat and proto-jungle sounds wouldn't prevail locally, he remains a local pioneer and legend of a magical period in the region's cultural history.

PAUL TAYLOR

There was a lot of music lost from the period of 1986 through to 1990, because there was so much coming out. Me and Marcus used to have conversations not just about house tracks that were made around 1986 onwards, but things before that from disco and the jazz-funk era.

We chatted about what made a record good, what made a record bad. There were really cool tunes that were never going to be heard because they were lost singles of the late 70s and early 80s. Retro (Taylor's long-running club night) was born out of those conversations with Marcus. It's hard to believe Retro's got so big, for such a small mill town in Lancashire to be gracing Sunday nights in Pacha in Ibiza, and all around the world. We were the first to put Carl Cox on outside of London.

We had a meeting and he said he wanted to do Fridays at Angels. Fridays were failing because the Saturdays were so popular during the Paul Oakenfold and Carl Cox era. We needed someone like Marcus to come along and say, 'I know what we need in a venue like this'.

When he took over Friday nights at Angels, I had doubts about it. But he smashed it, and I said I'll never have a doubt about what you say about music. Being a bit of a soul boy at heart I just couldn't hear what he was trying to project at the time, but he proved me completely wrong. There were people out there who thought like him, who wanted to be in the same room as him, who wanted to dance to the music he was playing. He was an amazing guy.

I sometimes used to ask Marcus to play at the end of the night where it deserved to be a bit harder, and he'd play Belgian techno and stuff like that. It was just absolutely right for that time, and he used to smash it.

Marcus was part of the musical awareness of that whole generation. We didn't always agree on what was right and wrong for Angels, but we had one thing in common – a huge love of music, dance music. He proved that by going off and creating his world based around his belief of what music should sound like. I'll always give him huge credit for that.

The north-west was a catalyst for what house music went on to achieve, and we were a part of that movement. ”

angelsburnley
vision
friday 4 october
KKLASS
(rhythm is a mystery etc.)
vision masters paul taylor · marcus
massive 25k turbo sound
lazersprojectorsspecialfx
coaches welcome telephone 0282 35222 (subsidises considered)
door tax: £6.00 doors open: 9.30 till late
burnley its happenin'
design by wayne 0254 699989

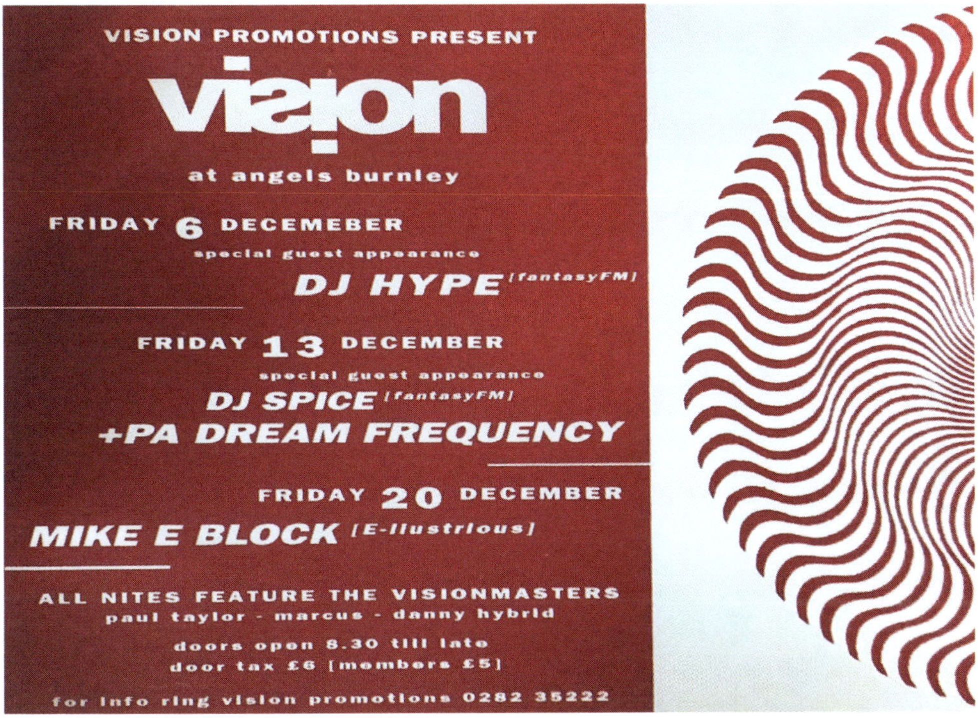
VISION PROMOTIONS PRESENT
vision
at angels burnley
FRIDAY 6 DECEMEBER
special guest appearance
DJ HYPE [fantasyFM]
FRIDAY 13 DECEMBER
special guest appearance
DJ SPICE [fantasyFM]
+PA DREAM FREQUENCY
FRIDAY 20 DECEMBER
MIKE E BLOCK [E-llustrious]
ALL NITES FEATURE THE VISIONMASTERS
paul taylor - marcus - danny hybrid
doors open 8.30 till late
door tax £6 [members £5]
for info ring vision promotions 0282 35222

vision
0831 151850
Friday 20th March
Dj Slipmat
Pa SL2
(Way in my brain, Dj's take control)
Friday 27th March
Dj Spice
(Fantasy fm)
ANGELS BURNLEY DJ MARCUS 9-2 £6

ROADS LESS TRAVELLED

> **Burnley's one and only… Big shout out to the DJ Marcus Kaye. This man knows the score, coz he is hardcore.**

MC Orchid, 1991 mix from Angels

Between 1988-1992, Marcus cemented his reputation as one of the north-west's most dexterous DJs, capable of keeping crowds bouncing regardless of setting – club, warehouse or house party. While less assured selectors clung to crowd-pleasing anthems, Marcus developed a distinctly singular vision that set him apart.

When navigating between peak-time bangers, he guided revellers down roads less travelled with mixes attuned both to their energy and his artistic vision. He would also go the extra mile – quite literally – with regular trips to buy records and check out nights in Manchester and increasingly more often to London, making sure he was on the frontline of the flourishing scene.

Troops of friends and fans supported his bookings across Lancashire and beyond – and his name started gaining recognition on the Manchester club scene. In spring 1991, he played on Sunset 102 FM, the Manchester-based pirate radio station that he'd once tuned into as a fan. Regular hosts included 808 State, and Mix Factory, who featured on bills with Marcus at Angels in Burnley.

PAUL HORNSBY

“ **He'd do a gig in Manchester, Newcastle, Leeds and we'd go there for a one-off night.**

We followed him round – he didn't have a huge following but those who knew, knew. At the time it was pure fun. Madness. Looking back on it, you get nostalgic. When we were living it, it felt like a lifetime. But it was a relatively short space of time, the Blackburn parties and all that. Then police broke it up, and then Salford, Moss Side all kicked off... ”

SOUND OF THE UNDERGROUND

The north-west had a thriving party scene in the early 90s, and while parts of the Midlands and further south were latching onto darker, breakbeat sounds, the region embraced euphoric music like Italo house, filled with upbeat, energetic piano riffs.

Marcus wasn't on board with music moving in a 'happier' direction; it wasn't aligned with his own tastes or style. His natural progression from the morose sounds of Factory Records to early acid house and Belgian techno led him to gravitate towards the darker sounds coming through, sticking to his mantra of playing music he liked rather than following the more commercial direction that dance music was heading in the north.

This mindset of being true to his beliefs rather than chasing fame or selling out became a badge of honour, and a reflection of what he thought the music could and should aspire to. Some of the music that was cutting-edge three years previously had already become cloned to death and commercialised, limiting its creative possibilities and leading to novelty records in the charts. Smart E's 'Sesame's Treet' and Urban Hype's 'Trip to Trumpton' summed up the direction. Pairing hardcore breakbeats and piano riffs with kids' TV rhymes, they both rode the wave to the top ten in the UK charts.

Meanwhile, he'd bagged himself a job at Manchester Underground Records, one of the city's leading record shops for upfront dance music. This firmly planted Marcus in the inner circle of the Manchester club scene as both participant and student. His pay supported an exploding and expensive vinyl addiction, but the insider knowledge he gained proved invaluable.

Situated on Fennel Street in the city centre, the shop was near to the legendary Konspiracy nightclub, which opened its doors in 1989 and hosted some of the country's leading talents and innovators in music. Marcus had got to know the promoters, the Jam MCs, through the party scene. Made up of Chris Jam and Tomlin, they had a strong rep for wowing crowds with their combination of mixing and toasting at the notorious Kitchen squat parties in Hulme, Blackburn raves and eventually Konspiracy.

On one occasion in 1990, the Jam MCs were playing at a warehouse rave in Nelson, Lancashire, a neighbouring town to Burnley. Like the rest of the area, it was littered with disused warehouses and mills that were prime locations for mass gatherings. Gilly remembers Marcus asking for a go on the decks to which the Jam MCs obliged. 'I stood behind him helping out with the sound,' Gilly recalls. 'He went on in front of thousands and he was brilliant.'

JACK FROST

"They were these big guys from Manchester, and we were just kids in Burnley playing records. But Marcus looked past that."

The Jam MCs must have taken note as Marcus worked the decks, confirming his place as a rising peer rather than a pretender out of his depth. He would play at Konspiracy nightclub and cross paths with them at other nightspots over the coming years.

PAUL HORNSBY

“The Jam MCs had him on at a number of nights in Manchester. Sometimes we’d be the only white people in the room.

This was the Cheetham Hill / Moss Side days, and Konspiracy and Home were known as moody clubs. But everyone respected Marcus, and because we were there with the guys who put the nights on, it was sound. We grew up in a generation when people were into the music, not the aggro. No mischief, we just wanted to have fun.”

THE MANAGEMENT OF KONSPIRACY
WISH 2 TAKE THIS OPPORTUNITY
TO THANK ALL THOSE WHO HAVE
SUPPORTED US SO FAR IN OUR
XCITING VENTURE IN2 THE FUTURE.

WE BELIEVE KONSPIRACY IS NOW
ESTABLISHING ITSELF AS THE WAY
4WARD IN KLUBLAND.
WE TRUST U ALL AGREE!.

ANY KONSTRUKTIVE KRITICISM OR
INDEED NEW IDEAS
ARE STILL WELCOME.

U HAVE NOW XPERIENCED THE FUTURE.
DON’T LOOK BACK

LET THE RAVE LIVE ON IN THE 90’s!

55 FENNEL STREET MANCHESTER M4 3D TEL: 061 832 9958

RAGE AGAINST THE LIGHT

Marcus first journeyed down to seminal London club night Rage in the early 1990s; it was to be as important as his first visits to the Haç. At Heaven, Fabio and Grooverider's explosive hybrid sets represented another genesis moment – the big bang of hardcore breakbeat and jungle that ultimately produced drum & bass.

Rage, which was held in the multi-room gay club Heaven, welcomed ravers, b-boys, gangsters, and celebrities alike, creating a space for febrile musical experimentation. This celebration of individualism and innovation spoke to Marcus.

Just as house music first expanded his adolescent mind, this glimpse into breakbeat futurism realigned Marcus's reality once more. The acid house eruption and the rave scene both redefined sound's existing strictures and now this latest UK mutation synthesised his influences into an intense and intoxicating strain.

Unlike the stunned 16-year-old struggling to process the Haçienda's cultural significance, Marcus was better prepared to understand Rage's pivotal role. No longer a spectator but a practitioner, he recognised Fabio and Grooverider's importance – true trailblazers unafraid to trust their instincts above following what was currently popular on the dancefloor. The experience in London was critical to Marcus's development as a DJ; it confirmed the feelings he had about the future direction of the music and made him more militant about his role within it. He wasn't alone: Kemistry & Storm and Goldie were among those inspired by trips to Rage.

JACK FROST

That club influenced Marcus. Just like that, he was like, 'I'm not doing *that* anymore, I'm doing *this.*' A lot of clubs didn't like it. But Marcus decided he had seen the light after Rage – and it was dark.

The temptation was there for Marcus to move to London and be amongst this energy, but he didn't. He had a girlfriend, Annabel, a solid group of mates that was expanding in different directions, and a life as a DJ and record dealer. He was perfectly positioned to champion the sounds he was hearing at Rage in the north.

The new sound of jungle music was divisive to his friends, and it signalled a schism in the scene. Jungle was a faster, streetwise offshoot of rave music, characterised by hyperkinetic breakbeats and cavernous low-end sub-bass. Its much-used Amen break, originally lifted from soul/funk band The Winston Brothers and caned by hip-hop producers like Mantronix, and its magpie approach to mangling everything from movie soundtracks to Jamaican reggae vocals and rare grooves, dub sirens and spaced out effects was the sound of generations of black music and culture. This was bottled into a uniquely UK invention. It brought black, Asian and white young ravers together on the dancefloor, creating a melting pot where heads from inner city estates could shack out next to posh kids from the suburbs. Society's barriers were being levelled. It was a cultural exchange that was a life-changing experience.

Naysayers – including many in the mainstream dance music press – viewed it as an aggressive mutation that strayed too far from house and techno's more palatable templates. The complex rhythms, time-stretched snares, and darker vibes jarred with those chasing the happy euphoria of earlier rave anthems. In its very essence, jungle had its roots in soundsystem culture, which had been under attack by the British establishment ever since the Windrush generation brought it to UK shores, and as a result, it was tagged with racist stereotypes from early on.

DJ FLIGHT

"Literally everything you can identify as jungle or drum & bass comes from Jamaican soundsystem culture.

From the use of soundsystems and ensuring speaker boxes emit a heavy and clean sound; DJs selecting tunes and MCs toasting or hosting proceedings (although the term deejay was previously used by people on the mic, riding the beat); to dub-plate culture and the friendly rivalry in trying to collect as many 'one aways' as possible; producing your own or being given special or VIP versions of tunes; rewinds/reloads (aka forwards) and banging walls or making noise to call for them. The way music itself is made! Using FX like delays, reverb, dropping out sections of a beat. Fashion, style, swagger. The language, slang or phrases that come from Patois, such as 'puuuuuuull uuuuuup,' 'skanking,' etc. Tune reactions like gun fingers, 'screwface'."

From *Resident Advisor's* RA Podcast – 'RA.942 DJ Flight' (2024)

For Marcus everything changed; it diverted him from DJing techno and house, and set him on course to start producing music. Rave was being commodified, whereas jungle revelled in its renegade reputation.

Back up north, Marcus was booking and playing alongside Hype, Shut Up & Dance, Micky Finn, Kenny Ken, Doc Scott and Grooverider – key instigators who put a flame under a niche southern scene and turned it into a full-blown youth movement. Marcus's mind was made up: this is the music he'd champion and promote in his DJ sets – even if it wasn't popular among some of his peers and the regulars on his dancefloors.

MARCUS

“That’s what excited me in the early 90s – the music coming out of London. A lot of it was white label stuff, you had no idea what it was, but it was all inspired by people being into the same DJs.

The London sound was so different to the north. I felt like I was on my own at times. Especially when I was doing the Blackburn parties and parties in Burnley. I was being pulled in that direction. Literally everyone else just wanted to hear Italian house music, hands in the air, vocals, you know. There was always that north-south split. When you went through the Midlands, got to Coventry and Birmingham, they were connected to what was going on in the south. As soon as you went up north it was a bit cheesier.

It started happening in the Haçienda too. I only remember it being good up until about 1991. Some of the DJs changed and the music policy did. Graeme Park was starting to play the US sound, the real vocally stuff, and the north went with it. It got happier and more commercial. People used to come up to me and say, ‘Have you got any E tunes’ – what are they? They just didn’t have any effect on me, I just don’t transcend to happier music. I always thought the moodier, more progressive sounds of London were trying different things; it just appealed to me much more.”

PAUL HORNSBY

"The thing with Marcus was that he could have sold out and become a celebrity DJ, like so many did. But he didn't.

I mean, back in the day us lot would go to clubs when Marcus was DJing and just emptying dancefloors – playing what he wanted to play. He'd go out and buy records and just play what he wanted to, and we loved it. He could have made thousands, but he didn't, he just stuck with what he wanted. He absolutely blind-refused to sell-out. I'd sometimes ask him, 'Marcus, why don't you play what they wanna hear?' He'd say, 'Fuck off', and stick to what he wanted."

CONNEXION
SALORA

GRAHAM 'GRUMPY' NAYLOR

"I used to drive Marcus to gigs over the years. We only lived a few minutes away from each other by car in Burnley, so I would go to his house and Marcus would still be sorting out his records for the gig.

Pat would let me in. I was always well-behaved in front of parents, very Kevin and Perry: 'Yes, Mrs Patterson'. She always offered a brew and I would politely decline. We'd have a quick chat about Burnley FC, which still goes on to this day, then Marcus would finally get his act together and we'd get on the road. This was both pre- and post-drum & bass. We went to quite a few far-flung places. We had a knack for going to venues that were dead, and if they weren't dead, Marcus would be killing it, and not in a good way – he really knew how to clear a dancefloor. I used to love it, because I got to hear the tracks that I liked. He never played to the crowd, always played what he wanted, which obviously didn't go down well with most of the punters, but got a lot of recognition from the right people.

I remember in the 90s when me, Marcus, and Paul Hornsby booked an 18-30 holiday in San Antonio, Ibiza. Our rep asked if we wanted to go on a pub crawl the moment we got there. We declined and told him that we'd only booked because it was cheap, and that we wouldn't be joining any of that malarky. Marcus DJd at Café Del Mar. That was pretty special. He didn't have any records, just those belonging to whoever was DJing there at the time. He got us freebie tickets for the opening night of Manumission at Ku, which was wall-to-wall nob-heads and the drinks were extortionate! We'd hired a car to do a bit of sightseeing and we'd pulled into a lay-by overlooking the sea. Paul took a very rare pic of me and Marcus together. I pulled out of the lay-by, reverted to driving on the UK side of the road, and soon realised that error about ten corners further along the windy road, very narrowly missing an oncoming car and sending us into the sea..."

A NEW DAWN

90s Manchester: a DIY mentality coursed through the city's musical veins. After Factory Records, the Haçienda and 'Madchester' exploded into nationwide consciousness, a city that's never short of self-confidence had extra swagger in its step.

The club scene, fuelled with a cocktail of substances and the promise of good times, had a tractor beam magnetism, pulling in thrill-seeking music heads from across the UK and overseas. An annual influx of 60,000-plus students injected fresh, wide-eyed energy to dancefloors packed with streetwise locals, out-of-towners, stay-up-forever partiers from the Hulme estate, and plenty of wrong uns.

A fiercely independent underground music scene thrived away from the glare of the mainstream media. From record shops and pirate radio stations to club nights and labels, the next gen of music makers, DJs and event promoters created the future with Akai samplers, dubplates, and dodgy antennas. The city's red-brick walls, run by the not-to-be-fucked-with Poster Mafia, were an advert for what was brewing in clandestine studio basements and sweaty dancefloors across the city.

Despite landing his first job selling vinyl at Manchester Underground, Marcus still made trips across town to buy white labels from Mark McKinley (Mark XTC) at rival shop Spin Inn. A part of the rave collective Mix Factory and winner of the NW DMC, an elite DJ competition for turntablists, Mark was already a credible force in the city and had the advantage of his cousin running the distribution network for all the key labels and producers. It was like a version of the sci-fi film *Dune*: 'He who controls the vinyl controls the scene.' And Mark was building his own universe.

MARK XTC

One day I said, 'Listen, why are you working there? You don't like the tunes (Manchester Underground was best known for house), come and work for me.' So I employed him and that's how we started.

After he'd come and worked for me at Spin Inn, we hit it off beyond belief, and we were basically inseparable. I'd drive him home in my Peugeot 205 rather than him getting the bus to Burnley. We'd get there and chat with his mum, Pat. And that's how we got closer and closer. It was a proper brotherhood. I call Pat my second mum. The thing me and Marcus had was that we were both brought up by our mums, him in Burnley, me in Oldham. We shared a love for music like hip-hop and techno. We grew up in parallel. It was meant to be.

I had all the music before anybody else. My cousin Paul (Higgy), who started Mix Factory, was the distributor for Music Mania. When a tune like 'We Are I.E.' by Lennie De Ice came in, I knew it was going to be huge. I took all of them on sale or return. We had 200 white labels just sat there and when we put it on it was four-deep at the counter and people are shouting: 'I'll have one, I'll have one!' We sold them in no time, and I called up saying, 'Listen, I need more.' It was a game-changer.

Marcus now had a powerful ally to steer his ascent on the Manchester scene, and they quickly established a reputation as the city's leading duo for the freshest cuts as the sound morphed at warp speed from hardcore breakbeat to jungle and drum & bass.

ATMOSPHERE
Issue 26
desire
foul play
metalheadz
Da Intalex
Nicki Blackmarket &
MC Stevie Hyper D

MARCUS

“I was working in Spin Inn, and that’s basically all we sold – the new jungle sound, and we were selling shitloads of it.

One title we could get 100 in and sell out in a week. The demand for the nights was there, we just couldn’t get anything together. Clubs just didn’t want it because of the fear of the type of people it would bring... it was rough, it was dangerous, so you could appreciate where they were coming from. But as a DJ it was impossible. People wanted it in Manchester, they didn’t in Burnley. It just took years to get going.”

Having the hottest records and music to play before anyone else gave them a serious amount of clout over other DJs. They were soon offered another piece of what was becoming a mini-empire. Norman Jay and Gordon Mac headed north to launch their Kiss FM station in Manchester, with Mark and Marcus offered the chance to host the jungle/drum & bass show in late 1994. Going out live every Monday evening between 8-10pm on 102 FM, it was only a small twist away on the dial from reggae specialists Frontline FM, an unlicensed pirate station who broadcast out of the Moss Side area. Kiss had started life as a pirate before getting its licence, and Mark and Marcus had previously spun on another – Sunset 102 FM. The close proximity on the dial was a metaphor for the blurry lines between what was legal or not.

The show became as essential listening to fans of the genre as Radio 1’s ‘One in the Jungle’. If anything, it received more love due to it being made in Manchester by two leaders of the scene, who you could go and have a natter with and buy records from the next day.

From a studio on the Portland Street / Oxford Street axis, just up the road from the BBC’s original northern HQ, the upstart station and its Da Intalex (the name they started using) show vibrated across the city and beyond, shaking Manchester to its foundations and inspiring a whole wave of junglists and drum & bass heads.

MARK XTC

“You gotta think of what jungle/drum & bass was doing between 93-95. You know, from that point, the whole scene and industry changed. You could make a jungle tune, and if it blew up, it was gonna chart. Because of that, they just let us do what we wanted.”

MARCUS

“The first couple of shows I was nervous as hell. You're on Kiss, you've hit the big time, and you're some kid from Burnley with a northern accent thinking you sound stupid. Because we were there at 8pm on a Monday, there was only us in the studio. It was a laugh. We used to make it up as we went along.”

The show was a sonic signal from the future – you'd hear the freshest dubs straight from their nascent Intalex productions and links in Bristol and London. Die, Roni, Krust, Lemon D and Dillinja, always Dillinja. 'Ja's signature basslines seared into your subconscious, never to be forgotten. Hairs on your arm stood tall as the bass throbbed out of the speaker, moving the air like the producer had his own superpower.

Something for Your mind

THOSE WHO'VE paid a trip to the Alaska bar, where the livin is easy, for Sunday evening drinks, there's no need to read further. You'll know all about how Messers Marcus Kaye and Mark McKinley, aka Da Intalex, are entrancing the joint with sonic landscapes carved out of deep bass and rolling drums, for the past couple of months. And for those of you who haven't yet shared their lazy Sundays, it's lamentably the only place in town, you're gonna get an earful of what's known, for better or for worse, as jungle.

Mark began his DJing life playing house, while Mark was strictly a soul man. But times change, and having listened to the likes of Goldie ("he kept everything going"), and learnt, and now they're doing the jungle t'ing for themselves.

Gunning like snipers, their latest releases, **I Like It** (remix) and the apocalyptic **Mercy** created chaos on dancefloors across the country while Roni Size, Randall and DJ Swift (Chill FM) have all tagged Da Intelex as names to watch, with Ray Keith booking them for remixes. You can also absorb their shimmering mixes on Grand Central compilation, Frying the Fat, which is unleashed on the nation this November.

"When I produced Mercy I just thought of something as manic and cast and furious as I could and it was a club smash as soon as I'd made it," Mark enthuses, letting rip a huge "waaaargh ! ! !", leaving no doubt that Da Intelex really are totally insane.

Although their name links them to the spurious term "intelligent jungle", Da Intelex are as much about cerebral drum'n'bass for your ass, as well as you head.

"We don't feel we need to be called intelligent, we just don't want it to sound too commercial. At the end of the day the main aspect of our music is having a beat with a bass that people can wiggle their bums to," Mark concedes.

Da Intelex' plates may have been thrashed in the clubs for the past six months, but their records have only just reached the shops, due to a manufacturing cock-up at PWL. Fed up with waiting, they started Jump Up Records to replace the former Intalex Productions and the first release, **New Dawn**, a quality slab of hardstep from Mark under his "X" moniker, is out this month. Plans for a label dealing with more laid back affairs are also afoot.

It's an old story now, but the struggle still goes on; gang problems in Manchester, further compounded by paranoia, means there are no consistent jungle nights in the city and Da Intelex' radio show on Kiss 102 is the only flame (aside from the pirates) keeping the WD-40 canisters ignited for the 13,000 faithful, who tune in each week.

When asked whether there is a solution to this problem, they just shake their heads and laugh, before adding, "The police will stop anything that's got something to do with the gangs and the gangs happen to like jungle; that's the way it is. The same thing happened to soul when they were into soul."

The gangs may be drawn to their music, but Mark and Marcus claim not to be personally aquainted with any. In fact the only resemblance Da Intelex bear to gangsters is Marcus's predilection for chicken burgers with extra mayo - heavy on the garlic, easy on the olives. Rarely is he spotted in the basement jungle section of Eastern Bloc, where he works, without a burger in his hands and he attacks a particularly large one with gusto as we speak. In between mouthfuls, however, neither Marcus nor Mark show any sign of giving in to prejudice or pressure and are adamant they won't be following Gerald to London

"London is where we'll make our break, but we're not going to do one and leave Manchester; it's where we're from and you don't abandon your own territory do you?" Marcus demands.

Manchester, are you ready for the rampage?

Rachel Newsome

Dawn Daniels

TUNDE 2D BABALOLA (FUTURE CUT)

I'd known Marcus since I was about 14. I used to go to Spin Inn to see him, Paul Walker and Mark XTC. I wanted to be a part of the scene and make tunes.

I told Marcus I wanted to start up and he gave me a starter pack. Back then it was a couple of floppy disks with the main breaks and samples on so I could get going and make tunes. Then they got the show on Kiss FM. The station did a competition called the Foster's Ice Breaker where you could enter your tune, and get it pressed and distributed. I told Mark and Marcus I was entering. Marcus, in his blunt Burnley way, told me, 'There's no favouritism so it better be good.' I played it, and he said, 'This ain't half bad.' They got votes in, and I ended up winning. From there he took me under his wing. All the tunes he'd take down to Music House (legendary dubplate cutting house for DJs/producers) in London. We knew no one, but he knew everyone in the mid-90s, like Fabio, Grooverider, Andy C. He'd introduce us to everyone. He did a lot for young talent.

Across the Peaks in Huddersfield, L Double was flying the junglist flag and taking notice. He was part of a secret network of regional champions, including SS in Leicester, Doc Scott in Coventry, and Bassline Smith in Derby. These pioneers worked under the cover of darkness in underground clubs and dimly lit studio bunkers, emerging bleary-eyed into the light at specialist record shops and radio stations.

As Mark and Marcus's reputation grew, L Double invited them to his studio. There, he engineered their first statement of intent, 'What Ya Gonna Do', released on his Flex label in 1994. This track put Manchester firmly on the jungle music map.

DA INTALEX
JUNGLE CHART 1994

01. Dillinja – *Deadly Deep Subs*
02. Roni Size & DJ Die – *Music Box*
03. Doc Scott – *Far Away*
04. Leviticus – *The Burial*
05. Conquering Lion – *Code Red*
06. DJ Peshay – *Psychosis*
07. Shy FX & UK Apache – *Original Nuttah*
08. Foul Play – *Volume 4*
09. Da Intalex – *What Ya Gonna Do*
10. Danny Breaks – *Droppin' Science Volume 03*

MARK XTC

"We got Mary J Blige's vocal, the drum loop that we were gonna use, the bass noise, and we had the riff. Double was our engineer because we couldn't engineer properly then.

He showed us a few bits in his bedroom and then we made 'What Ya Gonna Do'. Grooverider played it, Randall played it. I knew them anyway from playing at the Edge in Coventry, but they were superstar DJs to us. When we made that tune, we opened up all the doors.

Around that time, John Berry (co-founder of Eastern Bloc) came over to me and said, 'Pete Waterman's taking over the shop. We want to have two shops – the house and techno side, and the breakbeat, old skool, hardcore, jungle side with hip-hop.' I told Marcus what was going on and to come with me. 'Let's do this at Eastern Bloc.'

We went and spoke to Pete Waterman. I told him I wanted my own record label; I wanted to make sure we had our own brand. I knew the Eastern Bloc side was quite house-orientated, commercial, so I wanted to make sure we had something on our side, too. So we started the label, Intalex Recordings. Pete funded us. Basically, whatever tune we wanted to sign, he signed them, pressed the releases and did the marketing. All we had to do was promote it. We released a few tunes like 'Mercy', 'I Like It', The Outlaw's 'OG Call' and 'Searchin'.

I met up with people like Bryan Gee, Roni Size and all these kinds of people. We had all these tunes on DAT. Next minute I have all these DJs asking what this particular tune was. It was the 'I Like It' remix. Four tunes – 'I Like It', 'I Like It Remix', 'New Dawn' and 'New Dawn Remix' – set us off into the industry in 1994."

FLEX
RECORDS
DA INTALEX
WHAT YA GONNA DO
NICE & SLOW
5 028053 112018
ALL TRACKS WRITTEN AND PRODUCED BY
DA INTALEX MIXED BY THE DUBSTER
{ MARCUS X.T.C. L DOUBLE }
FLEX 001

THIS SIDE

INTALEX PRODUCTIONS

JUNGLE FEVER

Marcus and Mark ruled the roost in the basement at Eastern Bloc from its location on the junction of Oldham Street and Church Street in the Northern Quarter. The tribal nature of the club scene was manifest in record shop form at E Bloc: house and techno on the ground floor; drum & bass downstairs. Like Manchester's very own Black Market Records.

Second-hand specialists Vinyl Exchange sat opposite, and hip-hop heads Fat City were a couple of doors further down. Piccadilly Records and Spin Inn were to later relocate nearby. It was a record addict's dream.

Thanks to its cheap rents and abundance of commercial space, the Northern Quarter was the stomping ground of the city's creative industries. Unapologetically a bit grimy, it was an area buzzing with music venues, independent bars, skateboard and tattoo shops, and cheap curry caffs.

Musically, in the mainstream consciousness at least, Manchester was still living off its madferrit rep. *Mixmag* and others ran features debating whether jungle equalled trouble, and Oasis could be heard seeping out of smoke-filled boozers with sticky tables and blasted out by lairy beer boys and student wannabes with questionable haircuts.

Jungle/drum & bass was looked down upon by its peers – house and techno heads would openly diss it, and the truly deluded would disparagingly refer to it as 'poor man's hip-hop'. As a result, it became more militant, proudly wearing its outsider label and zealously defending itself. The disrespect pissed Marcus off to no end, and he had a reputation for giving zero fucks and speaking his mind – whether you were making what he saw as an unwise choice in the shop, or you were a DJ from another scene taking the piss out of the music he loved.

ST FILES

"I knew Marcus from when he worked in the Manchester Underground record shop. It turns out he was avoiding serving me, and I was avoiding being served by him. He thought I was an Italian house raver, and I thought he was some Belgian techno sort of guy. But it turned out we did have some middle ground: we both liked deep US house stuff, Masters at Work and stuff like that.

When he moved to the Spin Inn and worked with Mark, I took in some music I'd made with a friend on an Amiga computer – 'Motivation'. It was the first thing we made, and I thought it was easy. Mark and Marcus had made 'What Ya Gonna Do' with L Double and I was working with him as well at his studio in Huddersfield. He was connected to Unique 3 and the whole bleep thing. Off the back of their big tune 'The Theme', they'd built a decent studio with massive Tannoy speakers.

After Mark and Marcus got their grant from PWL (Pete Waterman's label) and built a studio in New Mount Street, that's when me and Marcus started speaking properly. I put my gear in there and they had theirs; it was still pretty basic. We had a speaker in the corner, a couple of Akai samplers and a mixing desk. One day Marcus was working on a track, and I started helping him with it. He wasn't technical but he had a real gift for what works and what doesn't. I think that's why we worked well together.

I didn't like it when people used to say I was the engineer and Marcus was the creative. I didn't think that was fair on both of us. I came from the more technical side of things, but I was firing loads of ideas everywhere, which isn't that helpful. You need someone to say, 'Let's focus on this bit, this bit's really cool,' and that's what Marcus did. And I did the same to him if he was on the keyboard. When we both agreed something worked, we knew we were onto something good.

We did a track together called 'Vintage Wash' (under the Kaos Theory alias, 1995), which came out on the Intalex label. It was a b-side, but Fabio played it, Bukem played it. We had a lot of fun, no set hours, just had a great time. Around the same time, we did the remix of 'I Like It', which made it onto loads of jungle compilations."

MARK XTC

Lee and Marcus used to hate me because I'd tell them which samples to use. I'd tell them that certain things needed to be finished tonight; I'm going to London to Music House tomorrow.

They worked all night on the 'I Like It Remix', and I went to the studio at 7 or 8 o'clock in the morning. Lee was still messing about with it. Marcus is gone. And Lee said, 'It's not done'. So I said, 'Play it,' and the bass note came in, and I said 'I'm taking it.' I took it to Music House and Roni Size cut it, Bryan Gee, Goldie, Leon (Music House), about ten man cut it, but they actually all wanted Lee's 'New Dawn Remix' and they cut 'I Like It' on the other side. It's only after they started playing it in clubs that they saw the reaction to it. It's the 808 bass, that's what made it different.

Manchester's stock was rising. But the city's gangland disputes were escalating and drum & bass events, as the soundtrack of choice for the streets and way of making money from the drug trade and cash-in-hand club scene, were in the crosshairs. It was a city where you had to be on your toes, and walking home at night in the wrong neighbourhood was asking for trouble. A dealer pouring petrol over someone for an unpaid tick bill, a random impersonating the police in the wee small hours, or clubs being shutdown mid-rave as bouncers stood in between two warring factions; it was all part of life on the margins.

MARCUS

"I remember people walking round with sawn-off shotguns at a place called the Lighthouse.**

It was so exciting but also scary as hell. If people wanted a rewind, they'd just pull the trigger. There was a label called Sound of the Underground Recordings from London and they came up to play. They put that Shy FX record on with UK Apache, and they were all hidden round the back, scared to death. 'What was that?!' We were all used to it, it had become a regular thing. People who had never witnessed it before were scared for their lives."

MARK XTC

"**When 'Gunchester' started there was an incident at the Darkhouse event (at the PSV/Lighthouse) in Hulme. People were shooting, you know, letting off because they were buzzing off the tunes.**

A girl got shot in the foot in the room upstairs because they were firing into the roof from the ground floor. It's crazy but true. Me and Marcus witnessed all that.* We played at a place called UMIST in the city centre. We heard gunshots, and we looked at each other while carrying big heavy record boxes with dubplates in. We just heard: 'Mark! Marcus! Duck down!' Then we heard gunshots spraying from a car driving past. From that point then I remember us thinking, 'This has all got a bit mad. Every time we play it kicks off. We can't really play the music we love anymore.'"

***Author note (Mark OD) – The ceiling still had the scars to prove it years later.**

Intalexual Healing

Tipped by such luminaries as Randall and Roni Size DA INTALEX are the latest act to free break from th paranoia surrounding the Manchester jungle scene

OVER the last five years, the jungle scene has produced an awesome roster of DJs and producers. Marcus Kaye and Mark McKinley, otherwise known as **DA INTALEX**, are two Manchester rude boys who belong to this new generation of drum 'n' bassologists. They listened to the likes of Goldie, they learnt well and now they're doing it for themselves.

Gunning like snipers, the duo's latest releases, "I like It (Remix)" and the apocalyptic "Mercy", have been creating chaos on dancefloors across the country. It's little wonder that Randall, Roni Size and DJ Swift have all tagged Da Intalex as a name to watch, while Ray Keith is booking them for remixes.

"When I produced 'Mercy', I just wanted something as manic, fast and furious as I could get," enthuses Mark. "It was a club smash as soon as I'd made it."

Da Intalex's plates have been thrashed in the clubs for the past six months but, thanks to a manufacturing cock-up, their records have only just reached the shops. Fed up with waiting, they started Jump Up Records to run alongside their already existent Intalex Productions. The first Jump Up release is "New Dawn", a quality slab of hardstep from Mark under the moniker of The X.

Plans for yet another label, this one dealing with more laid-back affairs, are also afoot. But although they've been linked to the spurious "intelligent jungle" term, these guys also provide drum 'n' bass for your ass as well as your head.

"We don't feel we should be called 'intelligent' just because we don't want our music to sound too commercial," declares Mark. "At the end of the day, the point is to have a beat with a bass which people can wiggle their bums to."

words **Rachel Newsome**
picture **Raise-A-Head**

'I Like It (Remix)' and 'Mercy' are out now on Intalex Productions. The X's 'New Dawn' is on Jump Up

Manchester's gang problems and the accompanying paranoia mean that there are currently no consistent jungle nights in Da Intalex's home city. Their radio show on Kiss 102 is the only official flame keeping the WD-40 canisters ignited for the 13,000 faithful who tune in each week. Not that the pair are prepared to give in to prejudice or pressure. They're adamant they won't be following A Guy Called Gerald to London.

"London is where we'll make our break, but we're not leaving Manchester," says Marcus. "It's where we're from and you don't abandon your territory, do you?"

A LONG DARK TUNNEL

MADRUSH MC

“ **Guidance, my brothers and sisters, Guidance.** ”

SONIC

“ **Along with the moodiness and the raw energy of the crowd, I remember that feeling of futurism at Guidance, like we'd walked into somewhere that was a portal to an alien world 50 years from now.**

Tracks like 'Proton' and 'Lokuste' were getting the biggest reaction. It was a really mixed crowd, all walks of life. ”

By the late-90s, Mark and Marcus's lives had started pulling in different directions. Mark had growing family priorities with his young daughters, their radio show (now under the more commercial Galaxy brand) was coming to an end, and they were made redundant at Eastern Bloc as the business went through a period of change.

For a while Marcus reverted to DJing under his family name, Marcus Kaye. His selector skills and ability to read a crowd easily on a par with the big-name acts brave enough to venture into the unpredictable underworld of Manchester's clubland.

It was a tumultuous time to promote D&B. Venue operators would instantly refuse promoters the prime slots of Friday and Saturday nights. As soon as you mentioned the words 'drum & bass', it was met with a shake of the head and the offer of a midweek slot at best. Flitting between Sankeys Soap and the Music Box, Guidance was the leading night to hear the big names from down south. While on the other side of the Atlantic rapper Talib Kweli mused about life in Brooklyn and 'getting murdered over a glare', you definitely had to watch your step at Guidance; the sound of people getting duffed up and taxed in the Music Box cubicles were an unwanted backdrop to having a piss.

Despite – or maybe in part because of – the undercurrent of danger, the night had an energy and intensity that was hard to match, and it was *the* place to hear the freshest dubplates. Doc Scott was a regular, and you'd often see Marcus and Scotty trying to manoeuvre through the heaving crowds to get to the DJ booth at the front – with one way in and one way out and sweat dripping off the ceiling into lukewarm tins of Red Stripe, it was a stress. But once in the booth, Scotty would always deliver. His signature sound of 'Shadow Boxing' came through like a sinister plague raining down curses on the dance. It was a masterclass in murk that left ravers in raptures. Randall, Kemistry & Storm, Andy C, Frost, Bukem, 'Rider, Roni, Bryan Gee and many more all waded their way through the Mancunian crowds with 20kg-plus dubplate-packed boxes in tow, sometimes two or three of those badboys carried by their entourage, ready to whip up dancefloors into a drenched frenzy.

In the middle of the hollering and flailing limbs, you'd see MCs Madrush and Diemond Ed trying to protect the mic from a host of wannabe spitters. And you'd have anomalies like Brian – an eccentric raver in a string vest who used to windmill his hands around and leap like a vexed ballet dancer across the dancefloor, right into the mushes of the hardest men in Manchester, a feat which often left them half-smiling in disbelief at the sheer ballsiness of it all.

By 1998, as the *Wormhole* tour rolled into Manchester on a dank autumnal night, Marcus played a near-perfect warm-up set before Ed Rush & Optical, edging up the energy levels and finally unleashing Ram Trilogy's 'No Reality' – a devastating blow that left the crowd on the verge of hysteria and calling for the rewind.

There was a palpable feeling that the Manchester drum & bass scene's time was coming. Future Cut and Sonic & Silver had joined the D&B heads in the New Mount Street studio complex and started to develop their sounds. Sappo was already well established with his Advisory label and dancefloor smashes like 'Ding Dong Bass', a firm favourite at the big raves. Producer/DJ Perfect Combination put out *Freeformin': The Manchester Movement Album* (1999) to project a collective vibe like Bristol was known for, but it quickly fizzled out as it had some notable omissions and people started doing their own thing.

Club night Spellbound at Band on the Wall and then Planet K played a key role in changing the perception of drum & bass in the city. Initially created to have a live band jamming as part of the line-up, it provided a platform for a whole host of local talent including vocalist Jenna G to show she was a star in the ascendant. Tonn Piper made his name on the same stage, hyping the regulars with his signature rapid-fire delivery. Mark XTC, Sappo, Silver, Longman, Deval and promoter Inkey were among those who featured regularly.

The in-house band saw, for a while, James Ford (later of Simian Mobile Disco) thrashing away on drums and Jasper Byrne (aka Sonic) playing guitar; both students with band backgrounds who were now honing their craft as studio scientists. Even as the night reduced its reliance on the live angle and focused on D&B and nu skool breaks guest DJs, it largely managed to avoid the moody vibes of previous years.

JENNA G

Me and Marcus were in college together. I've known him from the beginning of my D&B career.

In fact, he was the beginning of my D&B career, release-wise. He let me sing at Guidance, got me on my first D&B release for Soul:r. He introduced me to Darren and Tunde (Future Cut), Goldie, even DRS in Midem (the annual music conference in Cannes) on a college trip.

GUIDANCE PLAYLIST

01. Doc Scott – *Shadow Boxing*
02. Adam F – *Metropolis (Doc Scott remix)*
03. Lemon D – *12:01*
04. DJ Die – *Special Treat*
05. DJ Die – *Watching Windows Gnarly Remix*
06. Krust – *Soul in Motion*
07. State Logik – *Technologik*
08. Ed Rush & Optical – *Slip Thru*
09. Ed Rush & Optical – *Wormhole*
10. John B – *Pressure*
11. Mampi Swift – *Hi Tek*
12. Dillinja – *Unexplored Territory*
13. Trace – *Sonar*
14. Cybotron feat Dillinja – *Revelations*
15. Boymerang – *Still*
16. Absolute Zero – *The Code*
17. Future Forces – *Strontium Jazz (Dillinja remix)*
18. Ram Trilogy – *No Reality*
19. Ed Rush, Optical & Fierce – *Cutslo (Lokuste Mix)*
20. Jonny L – *Piper (Grooverider Mix)*

HOW YOU MAKE ME FEEL

GRAHAM 'GRUMPY' NAYLOR

"I once drove Marcus to Goldie's to pick up a mixing desk that he was getting rid of. Apparently it was an old one of Noel Gallagher's, at least that's what Goldie said.

We turned up at his house and he was standing outside his front door in his underpants. We got out, and I said (probably not being the first or last to do so): 'That's not Goldie Hawn!?' Marcus chuckled, Goldie chose to ignore it and in his best northern accent said: 'Shall we get bacon butties on f't'northern lads?' He invited us in and we were all nattering on in the lounge while his daughter was kicking lumps out of me on the sofa. We had been there for well over an hour and he never did get the bacon butties on... The desk was huge and only just fit in my car. I don't know much about mixing desks, but I'm sure it allowed Marcus to perfect his craft a bit more."

Not content with creating a ruckus on dancefloors, Marcus's production aspirations were firmly in motion. Alongside ST Files he'd struck up a fruitful studio partnership with tracks on Renegade Hardware, Breakbeat Science, Emotif and the D&B Arena album. In what was a one-time-only release, they explored the convergence of house and broken beat with 'Taking Over Me' on Hospital Records. Under their Ill Figure alias, 'Untouchable' b/w 'Style' on Suburban Base blew up, both sides receiving heavy rotation on BBC Radio 1's 'One in the Jungle' and in the clubs. 'Style', with its catchy horns, hip-hop vocal and a bassline so wobbly it made jelly look stiff, remains a classic Mancunian wall-slapper. Like the kids carrying Henry Hill's groceries home for his mother in *Goodfellas* – the wall-slapping was the ultimate sign of respect.

In early 1999, their aim was simple: make a tune to get in Scotty's record box. What they created became a scene-defining moment. 'How You Make Me Feel' was like a shard of light suddenly flashing away in the gloaming, a clarion call for those who wanted to embrace a deeper, more soulful strain of dancefloor D&B.

GLENN AI

"Soon after Kemistry passed away, there was a last minute memorial event at Heaven nightclub. I was a student working with Marcus at Eastern Bloc's Leeds branch, and he persuaded me to go with him.

There was all of this techstep music being played. And we were having this massive chat about how it was such a shame there was nothing with any musicality, soul, vocals, or breakdowns.

Afterwards, we were playing records – early Good Looking and Creative Source – back at my parent's house in Camden, and Marcus said he had an idea. And then two or three days later, he played me an early version of 'How You Make Me Feel'. I remember it had a different bassline to the final version. Scotty was always his number one to send tracks to, and he snapped it up. It all came from that conversation at Heaven."

As darkside and jump-up D&B raged away in the big raves, and 'sausagefest' was used to describe the ratio of men to women rather than a celebration of British bangers, 'HYMMF' was the antidote. Bringing a hypnotic rolling groove with an acapella from a New York house release by Creative Force, it was immediately picked up by key tastemakers like Fabio who absolutely battered it on his Radio 1 show and at his weekly Swerve sessions in London. As legend would have it, Goldie got down on his knees in a *Wayne's World*-esque 'We're not worthy' salute after hearing it. Manchester D&B was having a moment.

CALIBRE

“When I first heard 'How You Make Me Feel' it confirmed feelings I had about drum & bass and its capacity for beauty in the dance.”

DRS

“I know a lot of producers who use it as a benchmark for quality. Around that time, that tune was a seed. We've seen it with other tunes like Shimon & Andy C's 'Bodyrock' where it almost creates a sub-genre. It brought ladies back to the dancefloors too; it was the counter to everyone in Burberry caps.”

DOC SCOTT

“**I don't say this lightly – it is one of the most important tracks in drum & bass history. At the time it came out the music was incredibly aggressive and male-centric.**

I remember going into the End in London, and Bryan Gee was coming out, and he said, 'Scotty man, where's all the girls at?!' I knew what he meant. A lot of the events were 90-95% male. A couple of months after that, I heard 'How You Make Me Feel' by Marcus and ST Files, and I knew this was the tune that the scene needed. The kick and snare were militant, but it had those vocals and chords. It was a reminder to people: you can have vocals in your tunes, it's not a bad thing!

In making music, timing counts for a lot. Sometimes an album or a track needed to come out at a specific time. Look at NWA, Wu-Tang or Oasis's first album – whatever it is. The world just needed that tune at that time. And that's what it was like with 'How You Make Me Feel'.”

HIGH CONTRAST

“I heard Fabio playing ‘How You Make Me Feel’ on the radio when I was about 19. That was an incredible moment for me. Someone had made this sound that I'd had an inkling for in my head. It was this perfect, beautiful track. I felt like it was the beginning of a new era of melodic, soulful drum & bass.”

DARREN FUTURE CUT

“They had one mixing desk, a sampler and a synth. They worked that equipment to the bone. The fact they made tunes like ‘How You Make Me Feel’ and remixes like 4hero's ‘9x9’ is amazing. The equipment was so basic.”

That scene-defining moment signalled the start of a movement. Marcus and Files led the way by setting the standard for others to follow. They also had a healthy disregard for a-sides with each 12” release having two killer cuts that could arguably be the lead single. ‘Love & Happiness’ and ‘Dreamworld’, again on Doc Scott's 31 Records, reinforced their reputation for mining the deeper end of the spectrum and showcased a sonic palette that saw them raid their record collections to sample Philadelphia's First Choice and an early Roger Sanchez cut. While they brought a musical maturity missing in a lot of the high-impact but quickly disposable dancefloor tracks at the time, they maintained a clear focus on making music to bust up a dance.

MARCUS

“We build a dancefloor element first, without being cheesy, and then put a musical element on top. The beats and bass – they've got to have impact.”

Next, Goldie got in on the action, snapping up 'Universe' and 'Lose Control' for his Metalheadz label. 'Universe' was the middle ground ST Files talks about. Using a snippet of Vikter Duplaix's soulful tones from a Masters at Work track, it's the definition of soul in motion. The flip showed their versatility with a techier, futuristic vibe. It proved a deadly DJ tool.

GOLDIE

> **"There are branches to this oak tree which we call this beautiful music, drum & bass. Marcus and ST Files established new branches for Metalheadz when releasing 'Universe'."**

Alongside their own productions, they'd quickly picked up a reputation for being able to work their magic as remixers. Their reinterpretation of MJ Cole's silky smooth UK garage cut 'Be Sincere' was a major calling card, maintaining the track's warm and soulful elements and updating it to a D&B tempo. Next came a flurry of requests from some of the scene's most influential figures. 'Just A Vision' for Clayton Hines' Renegade group had a vocal harmony you could hum along to and still have people calling for the rewind in the hands of DJs like Bryan Gee. UK pioneers 4hero followed: '9x9' and 'Better Place' were a dream to mix and showed they were masters of sequencing.

Closer to home, Un-Cut's 'Midnight', which thanks to Jenna G's ability to shine in live settings, was a singalong classic in Manchester long before it became a huge hit for the singer and Future Cut. It received plenty of play at Notting Hill Carnival over a blazingly hot August bank holiday weekend in 2001, ultimately scoring them a big label deal. Marcus, who lived with Darren from Future Cut at the time, and Files delivered a DJ-friendly relick that again showed they could do no wrong.

HIGH CONTRAST

'9x9' by 4hero, Un-Cut's 'Midnight', MJ Cole's 'Be Sincere'... these were all so influential to me and set the gold standard of what drum & bass remixes could be, especially if the song was from a different genre.

MARC MAC 4 HERO

They did the Solid State 'Just A Vision Remix' and it was a massive favourite down at Dollis Hill (where 4hero/Reinforced's studio was based). I remember after working with Vikter Duplaix and getting to know his vocals, I heard 'Universe' and was like, 'Who's gone and sampled Vikter like that?'

And some of the guys at Reinforced got hot under the collar until we heard it was Marcus, then everyone was like, 'Oh cool, he's dope, that's all good, calm down.' Plus the track was fire, really nicely done.

I remember they enjoyed doing the '9x9 Remix' because it was different to a lot of things they were doing at the time, i.e. remixing more sample-based music. '9x9' is a composition of live music: string section, upright bass, piano, vocals, Rhodes, analogue synths and drums, which allowed them to get some real depth in the re-arrangement. I wasted no time and asked them to do 'Better Place' which I prefer; it's less polished but still sounds great.

They had 'a sound' and that's not easy to do. Great remixers like Masters at Work, Basement Boys, Steve 'Silk' Hurley or even the Neptunes all have a sound, a formula for hits, and M.I.S.T. (Marcus Intalex and ST Files) had that.

KNOWLEDGEMAG.CO.
NOVEMBER 2002

MIST

words: CATALYST

There are many elements that set drum & bass aside from any other music scene. The rate at which it progresses is one of these factors, which at times can be alarming, but is always refreshing.

In today's game a successful artist must be in touch with this movement and relish the challenges that it can create. Marcus Intalex is one such figure in drum & bass who achieves this and more.

WORLDWIDE UNDERGROUND

Marcus and Files had been planning on starting the Soul:r label since the late 90s, but bided their time until they had the sound they wanted to present to the world. Early signings included Calibre, Jenna G, Marky, Sonic & Silver and D.Kay. Not only did the music stand out as distinctly different to the era's ubiquitous darkside D&B, it set a very high standard from the off – the first release 'Play On Me' by Marcus and Files was an instant classic. It was visually different too, with the label's pared-down matt cardboard artwork looking more at home next to a deep house or techno release than the typical D&B sci-fi design. Marcus later reflected on the launch:

> **I wanted it to encompass the word soul, it had elements of soul samples in there... And I didn't want it to look like the usual drum & bass, futuristic spaceship, kind of techno name. I wanted it to be a bit more thoughtful, more mature sounding.**

soul:r
M.I.S.T.
Jam Hot
soul:r

All rights of the producer and the owner of the recorded work reserved. Unauthorised copying, public performance, broadcasting, hiring or rental of this recording prohibited.
soul:
M.I.S.T
Soul:r 001

All rights of the producer and the owner of the recorded work reserved. Unauthorised copying, public performance, broadcasting, hiring or rental of this recording prohibited.
soul:
Calibre
Soul:r 002

All rights of the producer and the owner of the recorded work reserved. Unauthorised copying, public performance, broadcasting, hiring or rental of this recording prohibited.
soul:ution
series 1 part 1
Various Artists
Soul:r 004

All rights of the producer and the owner of the recorded work reserved. Unauthorised copying, public performance, broadcasting, hiring or rental of this recording prohibited.
soul:ution
series 1 part 2
Various Artists
Soul:r 005

soul:r
M.I.S.T.
Soul:r 007

soul:r
M.I.S.T.
Soul:r 008

soul:r
D Kay &
Epsilon
Soul:r 011

soul:r
014
St.Cal
Red Light
Little Man

soul:r
015
Marcus Intalex
Zumbar
Temperance

soul:r
016
Calibre
Hypnotise
The Water Carrier

soul:r
019
Klute
We're All Dying
Come Back To Me

soul:r
020
Mist:ical
Just a Little Herb feat. Ras T-Weed
Memory Jog

CALIBRE

“Fabio had signed me to a deal, and I was sending him tunes all the time. He played one at a rave Marcus was at. He said to Fabio, ‘I’m fuckin’ off, mate’. Fabio played one of my tunes as Marcus was leaving and he said that he saw him turn around and come back up again.

It was a tune called ‘Feelin’ I’d written after my grandad passed away. I had sampled Lightnin’ Hopkins, I was into sampling blues in drum & bass. It gave it this weird, archaic sound. Marcus got my number from someone and called me in Belfast. We spoke a few times, and I said I’d come to Manchester to make some music. I liked him instantly; I’d never spoken with anyone from Burnley before. He had a lot of confident energy.

Him and Lee had done ‘How You Make Me Feel’ around that time. I never thought much of my own music, but Marcus made me feel confident in my work. I’m from Northern Ireland, I think there’s an inherent feeling of insecurity because it's so overburdened with ideological pursuits. I had no interest in that. I’ve never been able to fit in with people who do.

The motivating factor behind making music was escapism, so going away to Manchester to do that was like a dream come true. Darren from Future Cut picked me up from the airport and we went to Pizza Express. Marcus was playing a gig somewhere; he already had his shit going on. And I met ST Files too, he’s pretty quiet and humble, but we’re close friends. He was technical in the studio but always contributed creatively. For me to go and collaborate with these guys was great, there was no opportunity like that in Belfast. So it was a real privilege. We did the ‘Mistical Dub EP’ as Mist:i:cal pretty quickly on that first trip.”

Calibre's name was on the lips of every drum & bass aficionado at the turn of the millennium. 'He's got 300 unsigned tracks' was one of the stories that did the rounds, and it all added to the mystery that surrounded him as he'd yet to start DJing and hadn't done any press. In addition, Belfast, a historically tough working-class city divided by tribal lines, had no previous when it came to D&B. But the times they were a-changin'. Along with Belfast's main man, Marky and XRS were leading the charge in Sao Paulo, and D.Kay was creating vibrations in Vienna.

As the music's centre of power started to tilt from an inner circle cutting acetates at Music House in north London to pockets of producers sending files directly to DJs and labels on AIM (AOL Instant Messenger), artists like Australia's Pendulum and Noisia from the Netherlands were about to blow open the floodgates for the next generation. The emergence of music-focused social network MySpace and forums Dogs on Acid and D&B Arena meant heads could connect and chat across time zones. Drum & bass was going global, and Soul:r offered a home for its most soulful creators.

Marky started travelling to play in Manchester and the energy in the dance confirmed to those present that you were witnessing history in the making. Here was a Brazilian with the biggest smile on his face, who could lift up a turntable sideways and scratch like DJ Qbert mid-set. It was as if Outkast had written Sao Paulo's finest his own song, 'Ain't nobody dope as me, I'm just so fresh and clean, so fresh and so clean, clean!' Marky was that guy.

The mutual respect and kinship Calibre struck up with Marcus and Lee was to become musical alchemy, a trio with the Midas touch in the studio. Announcing his arrival on Soul:r, Calibre cooked up 'Interphaze' b/w the colossal 'Fire & Water'. Another contender for best b-side of all time, 'Fire & Water' showcased Calibre's love of dub reggae, expertly processing the vocals of a Carl Malcolm pirate radio classic into a ghostly echo, and pairing it with neck-snapping rolling breaks and a bassline that could take your head clean off.

'Mistical Dub' continued down the path, this time filtering a sample from King Tubby's 'Dub In The Right Way' (another Manchester connection as it was reissued by Mick Hucknall's Blood & Fire label) over the top of metronomic beats and a bass Tubby himself would be proud of. Like all of their output, it never lost focus on the dancefloor.

DRS

"Maybe it's the northerner in me – kick me down nine times, I'll get up ten.

By the time Soul:r was kicking off, a lot of people who had bad experiences with Good Looking Records were giving up music, but I was trying to get back into drum & bass. Marcus was always throwing me bones, getting me as a resident at Soul:ution. But he was also holding me back and slowing it – he knew the potential I had, but he didn't want to give me all the praise at the beginning, so I got gassed. He kept it humble."

DJ FLIGHT

"I first met Marcus at a Metalheadz Sunday session at Dingwalls. That wasn't long after I started playing for 'Headz.

I think Marc Mac or one of the Reinforced guys intro'd me. It was when 'How You Make Me Feel' came out. I loved his tunes, they were amazing. I think Doc Scott was playing, and, as always, he was playing tunes that no one had ever heard before. We kept in touch after that night, I'd send some tunes and he started sending me bits.

When he started Soul:r, he'd send me tunes on CD. I would call him, all nervous because I really looked up to him. I just found it quite hard to steel my nerves before calling someone like that and ask for something, even though more often than not, I would get what I was asking for. But yeah, it felt like quite a big deal for me."

ST FILES

"Marky sent us 'LK'. I thought it was amazing, but we were a bit scared of it.

I went to something afterwards where Bryan Gee played it, and it was massive. It was a bit too late then for us. Sometimes you should trust your instinct. Maybe it was too 'happy'. In Soul:r's sound there's a bit of the Manchester sound, and the techno from Detroit. A lot of techno DJs said they connected with this city."

unglist
Movemen

soul:r
SPECIAL GUESTS
MARKY
& XRS
+ STAMINA MC
soul:ution
FRIDAY 13TH FEBRUARY
RESIDENTS
MARCUS INTALEX
CATALYST
MC DRS
£10/£8.50 adv
doors open 10pm til 3am
Band on the Wall
25 Swan Street Northern Quarter Manchester

WHAT'S THE SOUL:UTION?

Manchester's D&B club scene was in rude health in the early 2000s. Nights like Spellbound, Viagra Fools and Squiggle De Mash had transformed its once troublesome rep, and garage and Niche bassline events had taken away a lot of the dancefloor tensions, leaving the true heads and a fresh generation of fans to occupy the floor.

MARK OD

"By the time Marcus and Lee set up Soul:r/Soul:ution, I'd teamed up with Wilf Prophecy and Silver to launch the Metropolis club night. It started with a bang: over 1,000 people came to the first one at Industry. It was pandemonium from the moment we opened the doors; people were bouncing off the walls.

Marcus used to pick me up for a weekly D&B 5-aside football game and hook me up with promos, or I'd grab them at his house on the way to the club. Afterwards, regulars would come up to me buzzing that I'd played Calibre's 'It's' and 'Mistical Dub' in a warm-up set, or 'Temperance' during the last hour. Metropolis was a full-on rave but all of Marcus, Files and Calibre's tracks stood out. They still stand out; they're timeless."

Soul:ution and Metropolis lit a fire under the Manchester drum & bass scene. They were joined by Audiosalad, who repped the headsier side, and jump-up specialists Platoon. Later on the Warehouse Project's Ape and Metropolis events would change the game, attracting arena-sized crowds. Rich Reason's Hit & Run, an intimate weekly Monday session, became a crucial incubator for new talent. It was a spot for the city's selectors to go as deep as they liked, with Marcus and Files' output a main ingredient of the wonky post-weekend vibe.

Quik

DJ BANE

"Right from the very beginning Soul:ution was on the cutting-edge, perfectly balancing the more forward-thinking, experimental side of D&B, whilst maintaining that raw dancefloor energy.

The regulars who attended were the most loyal, friendly and devoted music fans. They embraced music they had never heard before and danced from when the doors opened until the lights came on at 3am. They were also ready to catch DRS when he decided to do an impromptu crowd surf. It was a family vibe, attitudes were left at the door, and lifelong bonds were made."

SOUL:UTION
EARLY YEARS PLAYLIST

01. Calibre – *Fire & Water*
02. Jaheim – *Put That Woman First (Calibre Remix)*
03. Sunshine Anderson – *Heard It All Before (DJ Marky Remix)*
04. M.I.S.T. & Jenna G – *Lover*
05. M.I.S.T. – *Outer Space*
06. M.I.S.T. – *Dreamworld*
07. Calibre – *It's*
08. Calibre & High Contrast – *Mr Majestic*
09. Breakage – *So Vain*
10. dBridge – *Without Answers*
11. Mist:i:cal – *Mistical Dub*
12. M.I.S.T. – *Barracuda*
13. St.Cal – *Red Light*
14. Calibre – *Highlander*
15. D.Kay – *It's On the Way*

AL BAKER (SOUL:UTION PHOTOGRAPHER)

“

DJ Flight was on the first time I went. It was more melodic. It was more musical. It was more of a journey.

People could play at the beginning of the night, and they'd build on it throughout the night. It was at Band on the Wall – the spiritual home of Soul:ution. It moved around a bit but that was its home. The sound system and engineer was always great, it was all about quality and clarity, not just volume.

I got to know Marcus there. I already knew DRS from photographing Broke 'n' English (Manc hip-hop crew), as they used to open for everyone who came to Manchester. When I was photographing Goldie and Marky on stage, they'd sometimes be like, 'Who's this guy?' The other DJs and MCs I used to work with had given me the confidence to work so closely with others. I had a free pass, which is gold.

”

DJ MARKY

Marcus paid me something like £60 to come and DJ at (the first) Soul:ution. But it was very important.

I met Sonic & Silver, DRS, Jenna, Calibre, they became a family. They are my friends now, after 21 years. I brought Marcus to Brazil, and the Brazilian people loved him. He became very famous in Brazil.

One of the biggest tracks in the early days of Soul:ution was 'Barracuda'. The first release on the Revolve:r label, it was a masterclass in arrangement, with all the elements having a conversation, and a hefty wub-wub bass and infectious percussion that created an exhilarating dancefloor rush. Andy C's debut *Nightlife* mix CD on Ram Records brought it to the attention of fans who were chasing the hardest of hits – and it opened the duo up to a whole new audience, a musical connection that continued in the Executioner's sets – from 'Midnight Remix' to 'Temperance' and 'Outer Space'.

'OUTER SPACE'

Six friends. Fabric London. 2003. 5am. Lights on. Andy C rewinds three times. Amazing.

DJ Hillfinger, YouTube comments

'Outer Space' came at a time when Marcus and Lee were going through a dry patch creatively. Like many epiphanies, it was unlocked by a DJ dropping a certain tune on a sweaty and intense dancefloor, in a crumbling part of town.

Ancoats – except for the weekly euphoric carnage at the Sankeys nightclub – was a dystopian wasteland. Its decaying industrial mills eerily framed in the night sky by flickering ochre streetlights. Marcus made the trip on a night off and caught James 'Boggy' Holroyd – a DJ cut from the same cloth; a northern DJ who inspired legions of music lovers through his sets at Bugged Out! and Back to Basics, a selector who had a specialist knowledge and respect for Chicago and Detroit, and the man who teased in Bobby Konders' 'Nervous Acid' track as Marcus surveyed the dancefloor. Holroyd had form: it was the same club he lit a fuse under in the 90s with Jeff Mills' 'The Bells'; the perfect record to turn up the heat on an expectant crowd.

The kernel of an idea was planted. A few days later, 'Outer Space', with its futuristic, Detroit-inspired soundscape and unforgettable extended drum rolls inspired by Konders, was done and dusted – one of the quickest tracks the duo made.

DJ SAPPO

“'Outer Space' bridged a gap between light and dark. It was dropped in the middle of hardcore raves.

Brockie, Ray Keith and Andy C played it. For a period of time, Marcus and Lee nailed it. I think it goes back to them being there from the beginning of jungle. In the beginning, north-west jungle wasn't a big thing. We built it up, all of us.”

DJ FLIGHT

"When BBC 1Xtra launched, they approached Marcus first to do the Friday night show so that they had a spectrum of music.

L Double was doing the flagship show covering all genres, a bit more dancefloor; and then Bailey was a bit heavier, darker, harder; and then they wanted someone who would be a bit more soulful, deeper at that time. But Marcus turned it down. After that they approached me and brought me on board.*

Because he'd obviously been doing radio, like Galaxy and Kiss, he was well-versed in radio shows. I don't know if it was because it was a BBC thing. It was a Friday night and required commitment as it was live. It's difficult for someone to come down to London from Manchester, it wipes their whole night out. Whereas for me, I could still do the odd booking after midnight. But I still had to give up three of my residencies at that time – one in Frankfurt, and two at Fabric. We never really spoke about it, but he continued supporting me with music. I was playing everything Soul:r and Revolve:r were putting out."

Fabric, in a roundabout way, was to become Soul:ution's second home, the night regularly taking over the intimate room three. Marcus's increasingly important role as a connector of scenes and people led him to introduce a young Benji B to the club's event staff – a relationship that thrived as Benji became one of the UK's most revered selectors through his Radio 1 show and Deviation club night.

*Author note – Sappo also hosted a 1Xtra D&B show from 2004-2007

STRAIGHT DOWN THE MIDDLE

During this period, Soul:r, Revolve:r, and by extension Calibre's Signature, were buy-on-sight labels. Calibre collaborated with High Contrast to produce one of his finest moments, 'Mr Majestic'. Eindhoven's Martyn made his debut on Revolve:r. Like-minded producers dBridge, Klute and Instra:mental became part of a wider coalition, producing a deeper shade of D&B that was the antithesis to a lot of the disposable cuts blowing up in the big raves.

Rather than sticking to what had become a winning formula and giving people more of what they wanted, the next move was to signal a new direction for the camp and usher in a whole new wave. The release of DAT Music, an umbrella project dedicated to finding soul in the machine and exploring the genre's outer edges, was clearly influenced by Detroit techno's synth-obsessed originators.

It came at a time when dubstep's chest-rattling basslines had the UK's club scene in a vice-like grip. A mighty branch of the UK's soundsystem lineage, dubstep's fresh, experimental energy clearly caught the attention of adventurous producers like Martyn who cooked up 'Broken' for DAT Music. In doing so, Martyn cultivated fertile new ground at 140BPM that would see D&B, dubstep and techno heads, and labels like Hessle Audio, Autonomic and Hyperdub, coalesce to mine the deepest regions of bass music.

Marcus's contribution – his first solo EP – demonstrated his increasing confidence as a producer. The four-track 'Refreshed EP' contained the hypnotic futurism of 'Wide Eyes' alongside a title track that shimmered and oscillated with rising synth patterns. It was an example of D&B's potential as an artform; it had the power to make you feel both uplifted and wistful.

MARCUS

I'm a sucker for a bit of melancholy.

JENNA G

It ('Wide Eyes') should have been called 'Lost In Translation'. All I think about when I'm listening to it is neon lights, motorway bridges, Shibuya in the morning, fast trains.

Jenna wasn't alone in her admiration; a whole slew of producers were now, just like Marcus and Files had done with Scotty, trying to get his attention and feature in his sets. Up-and-coming producers Break, Icicle, Alix Perez, Zero Tolerance, Commix and Lynx were all audibly inspired by the vibrations coming out of Manchester.

In 2007, Marcus, Files and Calibre released their debut LP as Mist:i:cal. Their studio HQ was Marcus's home of many years, a suburban semi-detached on the border of Chorlton, Stretford and Old Trafford in south Manchester. On match days you could hear the roar of the crowd floating in the breeze from Man United's home stadium. *

*Mark OD: It was here I'd interviewed Marcus and Lee for *Atmosphere* as 'How You Make Me Feel' had started to blow up many years ago, in a modest first-floor bedroom converted into the source of many a classic.

Live
Every Sunday
at

ST FILES

“When Dom (Calibre) used to come over for Soul:ution, we’d head to Kingbee Records in Chorlton, and he’d buy a big stack of records.

We’d go through them and take samples. There was no set pattern to anything we did. When it starts to sound good, the energy in the room would pick up. We were just three people having a good time making music.”

For a trio who were anti-bombast and had a clear vision of what their music should aspire to, they were feeling increasingly confident in their message. This growing assurance was evident during their 2007 cover interview with *Knowledge* magazine.*

They’d already had the photos shot at Jackson’s Boat, a chain-y family boozer in the nearby Water Park, and were in good spirits, joking about getting a sponsorship from the pub for being shot there. The front cover, taken by scene photographer Cleveland Aaron, was a moment in time not to be repeated: the trio sat round a sticky table with pints and Calibre puffing on a cigarette, quite literally a picture of their MySpace bio at the time: ‘We are three blokes who drink beer and moan a lot.’

The Eleventh Hour featured notable vocal contributions from dance music royalty Diane Charlemagne and Robert Owens, and opened with a title track penned by MC DRS – a barbed cuss to drum & bass producers who had lost their way in the pursuit of popular acclaim. It didn’t hold any punches.

*Interviewed and written by Mark OD.

MIST:I:CAL FT. DRS - 'THE ELEVENTH HOUR'

Most producers these days, yo, I think you're cowards...
The same old structure that we've heard before.
The same old samples now you're out the door.
The same old bullshit drives me up the wall.
When was the point when you didn't care no more?

Soulrsig 001

Mist:ical – The Eleventh Hour

A, The Eleventh Hour feat DRS
B, Eject
C, Time To Fly
D, Mistical Soulution feat Ras T-Weed
E , City Life Feat DRS
F, Stay Away feat Dianne Charlemange
G, Amen Electric
H, Believe Feat Robert owens

Do not re - adjust ur lenses. Its finally here and due for release the first week of february.

Yes your one of the very few lucky people to receive this long overdue long player from messers Intalex, Files and Calibre, otherwise known as Mist:ical. Were sure u will find something on here of interest hopefully u will enjoy it all, but any support is very much welcome. There will also be extra brand new material on the cd which is due out at the same time.

For More Info, Interviews, features, contact Soul:r

e : info@soulr.co.uk

Distributed by ST Holdings

MARCUS

“A lot of the time we’re disappointed with what’s being put out there and some people have said they’re glad what we’re saying.

We’re not trying to have a dig at anyone. It’s just like, ‘Why does it have to be like this? What’s wrong?’

I love good drum & bass but the other side of it drives me mad. It’s a big disappointment. It also makes it difficult when people ask you what you do, some of the music is that bad, that lowest common denominator nonsense. Inevitably that’s what people think it is. That’s not what we make.”

In a scene known for defending itself militantly against outside forces and one that had adopted ‘it’s all good’ as a mantra for any style of the genre, this was a refreshingly blunt assessment of the state of things. The album connected with tastemakers outside of drum & bass, too. *Jockey Slut* founder and Bugged Out! promoter John Burgess gave it a four-star rating in the *Guardian*, praising it as ‘an innovative step forward that deserves to be heard.’ It was also to be prophetic about its future trajectory.

ST FILES

That's the problem with music: people are listening to stuff that's built to have impact and instant hooks.

The stuff I like best in my collection is the stuff that didn't have a big impact at the time but have become so-called classics.

Marcus, sporting his trademark baseball cap and peering over his specs, had embraced his position in the scene with an almost defiant zeal.

MARCUS

The thing is if he (nodding at Dom) doesn't do it (DJing), I need to do it, because who the fuck else is going to?

It needs to be done because good music exists. Not many people with a reputation as a DJ/producer offer an alternative. It has to be done.

This burning desire to spread the music far and wide also saw him back on the radio – this time switching FM frequencies for a pre-recorded Soul:ution internet show for Red Bull Music Academy. Delivered in his trademark dry and self-deprecating tone, it was like he was having a conversation with you over a pint rather than overtly hyping up the music. SunAndBass, the annual gathering of D&B's deepest heads in the idyllic surroundings of Sardinia, Italy, also showcased his reputation as a killer selector. His back-to-back sets with longtime comrade Doc Scott, where they sometimes delved into their techno roots, proving to be legendary.

DOC SCOTT

He was a fucking incredible DJ. It doesn't get spoken about enough. When we played back-to-back, his selections were unique.

The mark of a great DJ is making a tune that you thought was average sound incredible, and Marcus could do that. He'd do it all the time. I think I'm right in saying that he loved DJing. He could make great music, but he loved DJing more than anything. He treated it like an artform. If he felt like he didn't play well, he'd be miserable.

TASHA

We first met at SunAndBass in 2008 – we connected instantly. He had a reputation as being a grumpy sod, but he wasn't like that at all.

He was sweet, soft and gentle. Every person I introduced him to, he took such an interest in what people were about and made people feel valued. He's a Cancerian. The day after my birthday is his birthday. I do think we're a special breed (laughs). We have a soft, caring nature.

Sometimes you get producers that are amazing producers but not so amazing DJs. Marcus had it all. He always had the groove. He knew how to read the room, take it darker, keep it bubbly. He always had the sickest grooves.

Life on the road took Marcus and Calibre to all corners of the planet but the reality was like one of those memes of cold reality vs people's expectations of a glamorous international DJ lifestyle. While Calibre was initially a reluctant performer, happiest holed up in a studio for days on end making music like ST Files, Marcus coaxed him into it.

SOUL:UTION
RADIO PLAYLIST

01. dBridge – *Kismet*
02. Martyn – *Cloud Convention*
03. Calibre – *Deranged*
04. Lynx – *Uno*
05. Instra:mental – *Naked Zoo*
06. Jay Dee feat. Common – *E=mc2*
07. Saburuko – *Warped*
08. SP & Verse – *Lost Souls*
09. Commix – *Faceless (Marcus Intalex Remix)*
10. High Contrast – *If We Ever*
11. Commix – *Belle View*
12. Calibre – *Savannah Heat*
13. ST Files – *Moods*
14. Calibre feat. DRS – *Moving*
15. Marcus Intalex – *The Sentry*
16. Doc Scott – *Tokyo Dusk*
17. Sabre – *Global*
18. Seba – *As Long As It Takes*
19. Lomax – *Too Real*
20. Lenzman feat. Jo-s – *Fade Away*

CALIBRE

“I don’t think I was ever someone who was made out for the stage, but I remember when I met Marcus, he lifted me out of that and put me beside him.

He had to go through my alcoholic tendencies on the road – he put up with some shit when we were in places like the USA, Australia, all around the world.

My conditioning for the stage for so long was to get pissed. A lot of the time it was trying to get rid of the last hangover. I had a lot of trauma in my youth and it came out while I was on the road. When you’re on the road, you become vulnerable. I noticed that with Marcus, too, we were vulnerable in those moments on the road.

We were flying out of Houston, and we went somewhere to eat. Marcus pushed the table away, stood up and said, ‘I fuckin’ hate this country.’ I knew it was unsettling for him, which made me feel better because I was fucked off with it. I fuckin’ hate pretentious bollocks, I have to run away from it. And Marcus was the same. He didn’t like all of that bullshit.

I remember this gig we did in LA, in 2008. The economy had crashed. Me and Marcus were not far off looking like the most unhealthy bastards from the UK, in this beautiful spot in the sun in front of all these healthy dancers. I just thought, ‘Why would these healthy, young Americans want to look at us?’ ”

Fast forward to early 2009 and Marcus had settled into his role as a standard-bearer; his approval on tracks actively canvassed from the scene's originators to the hungriest up-and-coming producers. If Marcus thought it was decent, you knew you were onto something. Equally, he was typically scathing on anything (including his own) that he didn't think cut it, simply calling it 'fuckin' shite'. He was a man of few words when it came to critiquing music.

On the cusp of his 'Astro Dance EP', he was working behind the scenes on Lynx's debut LP and recently had Factory co-founder Tony Wilson's photo as his profile pic on MySpace to show his respect after the great champion of Manchester had sadly passed away.

He'd also reignited a passion outside of music – and was smashing balls straight down the middle of golf course fairways wherever he could on his travels, something which was used as a theme for his first solo cover of *Atmosphere* in the spring of 2009.*

It was done one freezing cold morning earlier that year at the Grove – a luxury PGA golf course about an hour from London complete with a spa and a helicopter landing pad. Marcus had a connection with one of the staff, who provided access to the course and a buggy for zipping around. In his element, Marcus looked the part, and was happy and relaxed as he expertly chipped out of bunkers and putted across the immaculately manicured greens.

*Interviewed by Mark OD.

MARCUS

“When I was at senior school about 25 years ago, one day we went on the field with golf clubs as part of PE. I lived close to the public course that was cheap to play.

I think at the time it was about 60 pence a round. I really got into it and during school holidays I used to play every day.

When I left school, I discovered music, the opposite sex and alcohol and forgot everything about sport. For the next ten years, I got consumed by music and rave and I didn't play. I think ten years ago I started making money from DJing and stuff and picked it up again. It is a bit of an addiction. These days, that's my vice. A lot of people have a drink, whatever, I think I've found what I'll be doing for the next few years. I just think I'll need to cut down a bit as it's taken over a little too much.”

Marcus was still busy DJing, but there were signs, perhaps magnified by the passing of Tony Wilson in August 2007, that he was contemplating his long-term future and the management of Soul:r. As he peered over his glasses and spoke with passion on the importance of pushing credible music and remaining independent, he resembled Tony.

MARCUS

“I'm excited about it, it's a natural progression. I'm not always going to be making music; I'm not always going to be DJing.

I enjoy the office side of it. I want to see if I can do it properly. He (Tony Wilson) was such an influence on the way we go about things at the label. He did so much for the city. I don't think Manchester will have a more important person. Let's hope we don't go bust like they did.”

Wilson's fiercely independent label Factory was notorious for having world-altering creativity twinned with an open disregard for financial diligence. As the legend goes, Peter Saville's artwork for New Order's 'Blue Monday' famously cost them on each sale rather than making a profit. It looked ace, though. The Haçienda was also a money pit, draining away the cash the label was making through high-profile legal cases with the police over their licence.

Musically, the soulful early Soul:r releases had metamorphosed into a techier minimal era, with Lynx and Alix Perez's 'Allegiance' keeping D&B heads stepping on dancefloors like Fabio's weekly Swerve party at the End nightclub. While Marcus was a champion of the sound, as always, he had one eye on the future.

MARCUS

It's almost too deep for the crowd in places. It's got overly serious again, which is good because you need that angle, but I want to get back in the studio and bridge that gap between mainstream and deep.

There's a certain vibe missing. It's lacking a bit of emotion. It's a bit cold. I love a minimal track as much as the next man, but it's almost like producers are trying to out deep each other.

Whether intentional or not from the label founders, ST Files' 'Moods' track and Marcus's 'Astro Dance EP' encapsulated how the 'headsy' (as dBridge put it) end of D&B could maintain its ability to move people on the dancefloor while also containing a stirring sense of drama. All four tracks on the EP were killer, but 'Cabin Fever' with its ethereal synths, jungle breaks and warehouse bass, stood out as the track to make people wonder why they were feeling a bit emotional as they shacked out in the dance.

SQUADRON ASSEMBLE

MC DRS, aka Delroy Pottinger, was also bigged up in the Marcus *Atmosphere* cover feature and rightly called one of the best lyricists in the game. The pair's 2007 *FabricLive.35* release was already seen as one of the top-tier offerings in the club's DJ mix series, but for those with their ears to the ground, Del had been one of Manchester's most important storytellers for many years.

To understand what came next, you've got to rewind to the late 90s/ early 00s. Manchester's hip-hop scene was a hotbed for spitters, and Johnny Wheeler, aka Strategy, could go bar for bar with anyone, often burying them in front of live audiences with his quick-witted freestyles and impeccable flow. Strats represented the multicultural heart of the scene. Part Jamaican-Irish heritage, and Salford born and bred, he joined forces with DRS to form Broke 'n' English after starting out in another crew called the Microdisiacs with Konny Kon (later of Children of Zeus).

Strategy and DRS formed a brotherly bond, going as far as getting matching tattoos of their group's name on their forearms, and they developed an almost telepathic way of complementing each other on the mic, with Konny joining them as their DJ and third lyricist on some tracks.

Early releases and mixtapes, featuring guest spots from Tonn Piper's brother Bandit and DJ/producer/MC Chimpo, saw them spit about ticking weed, impressing girls, life on the breadline and trying to make a living as MCs in a city that didn't have a blueprint to follow. Their Jon K-designed cover artwork had the duo looking disappointingly into an empty fridge, a relatable scenario for artists across the city who were trying to eek out a living from the club scene.

DRS

> **All these rappers like Aitch from Manny who have big deals and all that. They might not know it but this probably wouldn't exist without Broke 'n' English.**
>
> All of this comes from Marcus and that era. It's crazy. People have indirectly adopted his way of doing things. These stories need telling.

You could hear stomachs groaning just by looking at it. Getting hold of the latest white labels or a fresh pair of Nike Air Max often meant food shopping came down the pecking order. Trips to Jamaican takeaways Buzzrocks in Hulme or Dougie's in Moss Side for a jerk chicken fix, when you were feeling flush, were essential, though.

Broke 'n' English were deadly serious about their music ('Tryin'' is one of their finest moments – it was supported by Gilles Peterson and blew up on 1Xtra), but they had a cheeky, wisecracking side. The skits on their releases are some of the funniest shit you'll ever hear – from calling out toploader smokers to jokes about the surrealness of being a big-in-the-hood rapper while signing on at the Jobcentre. Chimpo, who could be found hustling his own *Feed The Chimp* mix-tape around town, showed his versatility by producing tracks and contributing memorable lyrics like, 'I'm watching so much telly, I think I'm falling in love with Lorraine Kelly.'

After their reputation escalated on the club scene and through releases on their own Estate Recordings label, highly respected Manchester label and record shop Fat City picked up *Subject 2 Status* for an album deal. Unfortunately, it didn't receive the love it deserved beyond Manchester and clued-up UK hip-hop fans, leaving the door open for a range of solo projects and wider collabs.

All of the extended Broke 'n' English squad were checking out jungle and D&B nights as far back as Spellbound in the late 90s, and when half-time D&B started to become a thing in the late 00s, the scene was set for them to crossover.

STRATEGY

I used to go to Soul:ution nights before I actually met Marcus. DRS was my guy. He was the one who introduced me into this world.

I was more into the rap side of things, but I was into jungle too. That's the thing about Manchester; it's a melting pot for culture. What was a tipping point for me was seeing DRS doing the half-time thing. My lyrics transitioned into that easily so it opened up a whole new world for me.

When I had my first release on Soul:r with Dub Phizix, 'The Editor' in 2011, it was a massive thing for me – it still is. It was a stepping stone in my career, and an introduction to a family. That's what Marcus was strong at – he would get a lot of community around him.

2011 signalled a boom time for lyricists in D&B. Dub Phizix and Strategy joined forces with Skeptical for 'Marka' – a moody half-time stepper that provided the foundations for Strategy to go sick with his enunciated Patois meets Costa Del Salford delivery. Its success took the duo around the world and back, causing chaos wherever they turned up, and announced Dub Phizix as a top-tier producer. Having spent his formative years on the dancefloor at Soul:ution and being schooled by Future Cut in the studio, it wasn't an overnight thing; it had been years in the making.

Fox, Skittles and Chunky, who had paid their dues in clubs across the city, were also finding the blurring of lines between genres suited their distinctive voices. 'Never Been' by Dub Phizix feat. Fox was a particular highlight, pairing the producer's razor-sharp beats and dancehall leanings with Fox's unmistakable mystical badman flow. The video featured Dub Phizix and Chimpo messing about in karate outfits, and like 'Marka', where Strats dressed up as a Native American shaman and somehow managed to rhyme marijuana, piranha, banana and drama into a visual narrative, they stood out for not giving a fuck.

In a scene where moody photo shoots had been the standard since day dot, these larger than life on-screen characters showed they weren't afraid to have a laugh while making seriously heavyweight bass music.

'Marka' and 'Never Been' ended up on dBridge's Exit and Kasra's Critical respectively, two labels putting in the work to redefine the genre's lines. Marcus gave his co-sign by picking up the Dub Phizix-produced 'Creator EP', feat. Strategy, Fox and Chimpo. Along with DRS, Soul:r now had an extended pool of Mancunian talent to call upon.

As Marcus continued to support and champion the next generation coming through, he'd made his home in Urmston, a village-y south Manchester suburb which had less hype and offered better value than Chorlton. He was spending hours upon hours in a converted attic studio and was ready to unleash a landmark project. After two decades in the game, it was time for his debut album, *21*.

A distillation of his influences dating back to warehouse raves and early house and techno across 13 tracks, it included collabs with garage music legend Zed Bias, who had relocated to Manchester, and a standout track with Brazil's S.P.Y. on 'Celestial Navigation'. Showcasing his increasing desire to be unshackled from making what people expected and to explore new tempos and genres, several tracks made a handbrake turn away from the drum & bass fast lane. The most memorable was a brooding cut called 'Dusk'. With its dystopian chords, it's a chilling listen that could be the soundtrack to walking around Ancoats at night in the 90s.

Encouraged by Marcus, DRS had also been hard at work in countless smoke-filled sessions and was ready to release his debut album on Soul:r. *I Don't Usually Like MCs, But...* showcased his versatility and poet-like penmanship as he sang and rapped across a range of tempos and styles. Forward-thinking producers dBridge, Enei from Saint Petersburg and Lenzman from the Netherlands were among the contributors. The album included a D&B entry point for multi-hyphenate Tyler Daley, aka Hoodman, who Strategy called 'the voice of an angel in a Sprayway jacket'. Tyler would later form soul/rap act Children of Zeus with Konny Kon, and sing his heart out alongside DRS on the emotionally-charged 'The View' feat. LSB.

The newly collaborative spirit, which hadn't always been the case in the city's competitive scene, was best exemplified by the posse cut, 'Bun Ya'. Featuring the voices of six of DRS's closest collaborators over an ominous Dub Phizix beat, it was a sign of things to come. As Tyler later said about DRS: 'He's the glue that holds us all together.'

RETURN TO THE SOURCE

MARCUS

“House was the first thing, but it was the sound of Detroit that got my full attention.

It was when that sound started to come back, sounding like it did when I was first into it, that I was like, ‘Hold on a minute, this is really exciting.’ Do you know what I mean? People moved away from the sort of dubstep thing to a merge of everything at once, and that’s how I remembered the early 90s to be. As far as DJing goes, that was probably the most exciting time for me. No other life distractions, just being a young 20-year-old, wanting to get into music as much as possible.”

ST FILES

“Funnily enough, I think I had started making house music initially. When I had my studio set up, Marcus came round, and I played some for him. I think when he heard my tunes he must have thought, ‘If this idiot can do it, so can I.’”

The release of *21* saw Marcus looking backwards at his earliest inspirations to push things forwards, and although it wasn’t the end of his drum & bass production – in fact, far from it – it coincided with an exciting new chapter of his career.

Under a golf-inspired new pseudonym, Trevino (from the US golfer Lee Trevino), he started to experiment with his first love – house and techno. His first release as Trevino was 'Chip' on Martyn's 3024 label, a powerful electro-charged cut that was paired with fellow D&B alumni Instra:mental's 'Pyramid' who'd been mining the deepest reaches of the dance with dBridge through the Autonomic label. 3024, named after a Rotterdam postcode in Martyn's hometown, brought things full circle; Marcus had signed his debut releases on Revolve:r. The former apprentice, now one of the most respected names in discerning underground circles, co-signed his former label boss and helped him navigate the transition.

MARTYN

“When Marcus was venturing into 'non-drum & bass', he was slightly worried if people would think he was selling out, or if it would confuse people if he used the name Marcus Intalex for both. Eventually he settled on Trevino after the golf legend.

He started chiselling away on techno, sending music to some people who still had links to drum & bass, like me and Scuba. He also put 'Derelict' out on NakedLunch in 2012. And then Ben Klock caught on and started bringing his music to a wider techno audience.”

MARCUS

“I didn't want to play techno gigs and have people coming up to me asking for drum & bass. That was the real reason. I'm happy for people to know it's me – that's not an issue at all – but it would drive me fucking bonkers if people asked me for drum & bass tunes in the middle of a techno club.”

TASHA

I booked Marcus as Trevino at my label club night Neighbourhood in the early days. I'd previously booked him to play techno as Marcus Intalex at Plastic People and some people complained, as they expected him to play D&B. He was always really supportive and loved the fact I was pushing techno that he liked.

I wanted to do a big party – and I booked producers that I was really into. I asked him to play with dBridge, Randomer and Alix Perez. It was actually a flop. We had to cut the night short, and I was incredibly embarrassed. It was near to Christmas, and I gave everyone a silly present. I gave Marcus jazzy socks that I later found out he wore so much they had holes in.

I was devastated that night. I said to Marcus, 'That's it now, I can't continue with my parties. I'm a failure.' And he was like, 'No, you can't give up, you took a chance on me. You didn't wait until I'd got several releases out and it was safe. You're just a bit ahead of the curve. Just learn from this experience. You have to keep doing parties.'

He's the reason why I continued. He had so much belief in me picking myself back up and getting better at being a promoter.

While the creative possibilities of producing at techno tempo had re-energised him after two decades in the game, Marcus was still producing drum & bass and was about to develop an important new friendship and label collaborator. LSB, aka Luke Beavon, was an up-and-coming deep-end D&B producer, who shared a love of golf. The two originally met in 2006 when Luke was promoting a 1Xtra night at his Bounce event in Norwich; Marcus and Flight played back-to-back with Stamina MC. They reconnected on the golf course, a setting that had become as familiar to Marcus as being behind the decks.

LSB

“In 2011, I was gonna play golf with a friend who knew Marcus. He had a gig in London, so we'd decided to play in Surrey. The night before, our mutual friend cancelled.

I messaged Marcus and asked if he fancied playing anyway, despite us not really knowing each other. I was living in Newbury Park in east London at the time, so I said he could stay at mine. He was playing at Fabric that night, and we would play golf in the morning.

My wife's a big drum & bass fan. She was like, 'Marcus Intalex is in our shower'. She was a bit fangirl about it. Anyway, we got on really well, just golf buddies really. On the first tee, he started talking to his ball: 'No, no, no!' I found it humorous, Marcus was a bit of an omnivert. Some people would see him as grumpy and insular, but he was actually a big talker and extroverted at times. That might be a northern thing.”

Golf was Marcus's escape from the music business. Around this time, he was playing a few times a week. When he travelled abroad for gigs, a course would be swiftly sought out. Golf had started to be a factor in where he'd tour, too, giving him the chance to play at favourite courses, or ones he wanted to tick off his bucket list.

CALIBRE

“He was always working, never sleeping, always on the move, playing too much golf. I found it amusing when he got into it. Whenever we were travelling, he'd connect with people who played golf over the music.”

Living a dual musical identity resulted in a particularly productive time. Trevino gave him the creative freedom he'd been missing in D&B. This wasn't a falling out of love with drum & bass, but rather an opportunity for Intalex to benefit from the fresh creative spark he'd unlocked. A quick flurry of releases in 2012-2013 – 'Redan' on close compadre Geoff Wright's Samurai Music, 'Cabal' and 'Mud' on Ingredients, and the no-nonsense 'Riots' and 'Hell 2 Pay' on Metalheadz – showed he was on a roll.

In parallel, Marcus was going back to his roots and referencing the music he'd started out playing at clubs like Monroe's and Angels. Shortly after his first techno release came the beautiful 'Backtracking' and 'Juan Two Five' on Craig Richards' The Nothing Special label, and 'Derelict' and 'Buried' on NakedLunch, all nods to some of his earliest inspirations. As producer Sam Binga eloquently put it in a subsequent *UKF* tribute feature: 'Some of the best dance music rides that bittersweet edge between joy and heartbreak, between rhythms that make you respond physically and harmonies that touch you emotionally. For me, Marcus walked that line to perfection with this ('Backtracking') timeless record.'

HIGH CONTRAST

“He always stuck to his core sound which was influenced by Detroit techno.

The only difference was the tempo and the structure of the beat, but he was getting double money for techno – the different economics of the dancefloor. I remember him saying he'd get booked to play somewhere like Fabric as Trevino or as Intalex, and he'd get paid twice as much as Trevino because there's just more money in techno.”

MARCUS

“Obviously ‘Juan Two Five’ was a nod to Juan Atkins. ‘Backtracking’ was a slight nod to Fingers and that sort of late 80s house…

It was all stuff that I fucking loved playing back in the day. That was the most exciting period because it was all beginning then. It was like, ‘Fuck me, what is this stuff?’ It was the beginning of rave, the Haçienda, all that stuff, so I guess you can understand why I'm so into it – because I saw it all. I guess that music's just been sat there inside me waiting to be made. And it's not original. None of it's original. But it just felt like it was the right time to do it.

What it's done in terms of enjoyment is that I'm loving doing techno, obviously, but I'm also enjoying doing drum & bass more because I don't feel like it's as much of a concern anymore. If that's the only thing you do, then you've got to be completely on point all the time and the pressure's always there. What Trevino's done for Intalex is completely taken all the pressure away to the point where I feel like if people don't like it, it doesn't bother me anymore. I'm just doing it ‘cause I enjoy it. I'm enjoying the studio more than ever. I could literally not DJ and just spend the rest of my life in there… If only you could make a decent living out of it.”

MARCUS

TASHA

TREVINO PLAYLIST

01. Trevino – *Backtracking*
02. Trevino – *Under Surveillance*
03. Trevino – *Defektor Dub*
04. Trevino – *Forged*
05. Trevino – *Playtime*
06. Trevino – *Doldrums*
07. Trevino – *After The Rain*
08. Trevino – *Black Cat*
09. Trevino – *Mosaic*
10. Trevino – *Eve*

THE VIEW

As Marcus found a fresh creative groove with his Trevino alter ego, his personal life was taking an exciting turn. It was during this period of artistic reinvigoration that he crossed paths with Ayumi Maxwell, a drum & bass fan from New Zealand, who would become a profound person in his life.

Ayumi first met Marcus in 2011 while attending one of his shows in Auckland. A year later, on a working visa in London, she saw Marcus at a Commercial Suicide night at Cable in Bermondsey, London. He remembered their previous meeting, and the two kept in touch from there, which kicked off a close friendship. Over the next year, their bond strengthened into a relationship and Marcus asked Ayumi to head north to Manchester.

It was music at 174BPM that brought them together, but the two shared a passion for all sorts of music outside of drum & bass; mellow indie and shoegaze acts like Sharon Van Etten and Angel Olsen. Ayumi fondly recalls listening to what some would call melancholy music at home, though Marcus found it more uplifting than depressing.

Their musical connection ran deep. Ayumi remembers Marcus playing 'Climbing Up the Walls' – a homage to Radiohead's original – from his *21* album at the New Zealand show she first attended. It was a moment so meaningful she chose to play it at his funeral years later. The two bonded over Marcus's wide-ranging tastes. The contrast between his public persona and private musical tastes was as stark as night and day.

At the end of Ayumi's UK working holiday visa in 2014, with no option for renewal, they faced a decision on where to relocate next. Berlin emerged as the best nearby option to obtain a new visa without having to return to New Zealand. Initially, the plan was for Ayumi to move there while Marcus remained based in Manchester to keep his studio. However, after shuttling between the cities a couple of times, the vibrant buzz and thriving music scene convinced them both to give residing there a try.

Having a new base in Berlin allowed Marcus to further infiltrate the world of techno, and feature at the city's best-known clubs. Appearances at rarefied techno temple Berghain followed, and revered selectors Ben Klock and Marcel Dettmann became members of the Trevino fanclub. The latter showered praise on Trevino's 'Doldrums' track, which was released on the former's Klockworks label. 'You can practically see the smoke drifting through Berghain's dancefloor if you play this record loud enough.'

MARTYN

“When he broke into the techno nights, he thought it would be very different to the drum & bass world. It's a much bigger scene and way more competitive.

There was this one DJ/producer he really looked up to, and when he got the chance to play with him it turned out he was a twat. Marcus was playing before him in Berlin, and the guy asked him to slow the music down and get to a different BPM because that's where his set started. In drum & bass you never do that – especially not to Marcus. If you're a good DJ, you make it work and do your thing. After that, whenever the guy's name was mentioned, Marcus was like, 'I'm done with him.' Once you were on that side of him, there wasn't any turning back.”

Darwin, a Canadian DJ based in Berlin, who plays the full spectrum of the bass music continuum, got to know Marcus during this time, but first became familiar with Trevino when his 'Discovery EP' came out.

DARWIN

"I thought it was the coolest techno I'd ever fucking heard. This was at a time when all the bass guys started making techno and it sounded so fresh compared to the traditional format.

All the Trevino releases – especially the early records – just blew my mind. He did a promo mix for *Urb Magazine*, and to this day it's one of my favourite mixes of all-time. It was the slickest, techiest thing I'd ever heard. It's basically like drum & bass rollers but techy, tripped out techno.

I was in Croatia at the Dimensions Festival. I had just met Tony (Addison Groove) in the aisle of a supermarket, and we hit it off right away. I kidnapped him from his friends, and we were listening to the Trevino *Urb* mix all night on repeat. We joked about getting the tracklist tattooed."

During this time, Soul:r, like many independent D&B labels with modest resources, grappled with the changing tides of the music industry. The double whammy of the dominance of streaming services and volatile social algorithms made it increasingly difficult to make a decent living out of music sales. But all was not lost: the label experienced a resurgence off the back of DRS's second album, *Mid Mic Crisis* (2015). Most notably, 'The View' featuring LSB and Tyler Daley became a singalong global anthem – its big bittersweet chorus was belted out by fans everywhere from Sydney to Sardinia. This wasn't a fortuitous lightning strike; Marcus had steered LSB and DRS over many years.

LSB

After a few times of playing golf together, I said I'd send him some tunes. He listened to them, and he said, 'I like them, but something's not quite right. They're not gritty enough, or underground enough. Just keep working on them.'

Down the line I sent him a tune called 'Leave', which he liked and offered to release on Soul:r. I was a massive fan of the label and had all the vinyl. That came out in 2014. Around the same time, he was playing Fabric, and me and my wife went down, and he played my tune. It was the first time I'd heard any of my music in Fabric. I hated it. I told my wife, 'It sounds shit, we've got to go home.' For some reason I thought I'd ripped off Calibre's 'Keep Control'; I hadn't but I had to leave and check.

That was the beginning of us releasing music and doing gigs together. We'd often combine gigs with golf; it was more about the golf than the gigs. If we were in Vienna, Manchester, anywhere, we'd find a course.

LSB quickly progressed through the ranks to deliver his debut album, *Content* in 2016. 'Missing You' with Tyler Daley and DRS confirmed the trio as a killer combination. Tyler – who was starting to make waves with Children of Zeus – was a once in a generation voice. Not only could he break hearts with his falsetto, he could spit bars and produce beats – he was a certified triple-threat.

Soul:r continued to attract – and sign – new talent. Its Four:Fit series was a showcase of long-time label associates like Seba, Makoto and Calibre, alongside rising talent including Skeptical, FD and Adred. Marcus contributed the amen-powered rocket ship 'Jupiter' on the series' eighth EP. It became his most streamed track on Spotify.

In the early part of 2016, Marcus had teed up his first Trevino LP on the Birdie label. *Front* was a masterful take on house and techno, and contained a sonic palette and vibe, like on the dreamy 'La View', that Intalex fans would recognise. *Mixmag* praised the LP calling it 'simple but devastating dancefloor weaponry.'

MIXMAG

> **Trevino brings the qualities of his other work – pumped-up tempos, intricate melodies, breathtakingly crisp beats – to bear throughout *Front*, particularly 'Black Cat's' chattering, Far Eastern-flavoured deep acid trip, the witching hour dark tech of 'Defektor Dub' and the emotive, grand Italo house of 'Bergmann'. This is 4/4 music with balls.**

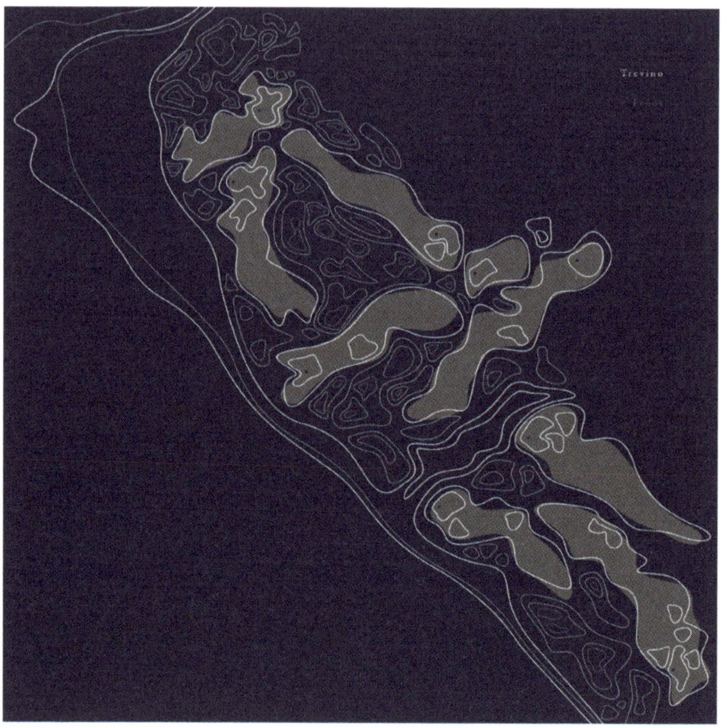

Front still stands up as a bold statement to cap off Trevino's first few years on the techno scene. Looking back retrospectively, seeing how his 'Four:Fit 008 EP' and *Front* came out within weeks of each other, yet again underlined Marcus's ability to successfully have one foot in each scene.

Later in 2016, Trevino released his 'Casino' EP on Aus Music, which was marketed as bringing 'together three deftly structured and dancefloor-focused tracks that blur the boundary between house and techno in true Trevino fashion.' The title track's piano riff could easily have been the base for a hands in the air vocal anthem, a tip of the hat to the early 90s sound, but in Marcus's hands it became a self-reflective earworm that stirs the soul.

DRS

I remember Marcus's tune 'Casino', I vocalled that. And it was fucking insane. He was like, 'This is *amazing*.'

All of a sudden, he did a U-turn on it, and he wasn't sure. After he passed, I spoke to a mate of ours, Will (Will Saul, Aus Music), and he said Marcus knew that would have been his biggest tune and he didn't want to be known for just that. I thought, 'What about me, the wanker!' Haha.

But that's the guy he was. Same with turning down DJ Marky's 'LK' for Soul:r. He knew that could have been a massive tune, but that's not what he wanted.

He could have let me burn bright for a short time, but he didn't. He taught me to be reserved and carry myself in a different way. MCing was all about being calm and delivered. That was taught by being patient.

Closing off the year, Marcus and Ayumi decided to come back to the UK after two years in Berlin. Marcus returned to Manchester, a city he had never really left with regular visits for intermittent Soul:ution nights among other gigs, with a newfound fanbase in the techno world. What had been a pragmatic move for visa reasons turned into a serendipitous trip for Marcus's Trevino adventures, broadening his ever-growing web of contacts in the music industry, and finding new allies among techno's elite in the Grey City.

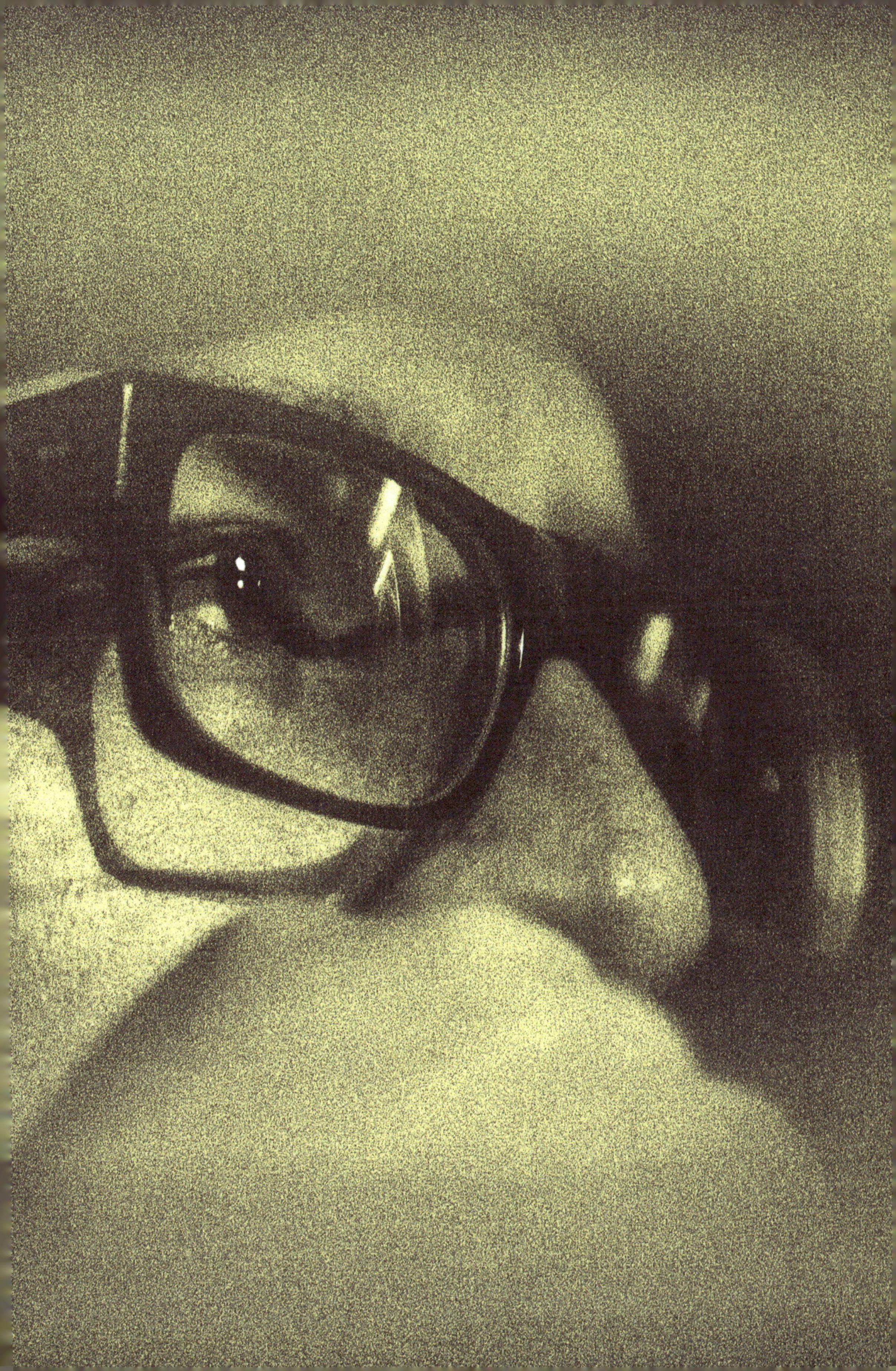

TRUE TO THE CRAFT

Marcus saw in 2017 at Disco 3000, a stamina-sapping 35–hour techno party in east Berlin, topping the bill alongside the UK's Oliver Ho and a whole host of local selectors. While he was in the process of moving back to Manchester, Marcus was still gigging in Berlin and across the UK, and in March he made it over to New Zealand and Australia, stopping off to spin in Dubai on the way.

A couple of months later, as captured at the start of this book, he hit a hole-in-one during a round of golf. For golfers, this is the stuff dreams are made of. You can play your entire life and never manage to get one. It was a day not to forget and he posted on Instagram to share his pride.

Just three weeks after this momentous occasion, Marcus tragically passed away following a Soul:ution night at the Soup Kitchen, Manchester. The devastating news sent shockwaves through the music world. Manchester based DJ/producer Antagonist and Soul:ution resident Bane were both there that night.

BANE

"The club was packed and rocking, all of the regular heads were there (front right as standard), and there were plenty of new young faces.

As usual, Marcus stole the show and absolutely destroyed the place. Marcus's set was packed full of Soul:ution classics and brand new material. At the peak of his set he dropped 'International', a fresh release from Spirit (RIP). Rewinds were called for, and of course Marcus obliged!"

ANTAGONIST

“Escher from Blocks & Escher was meant to go on after Marcus, but his USB was fucking up, so he had to go into the back and sort it out.

This meant Marcus had to do an unplanned extended set, and it was the sickest set I'd seen in years. He just nailed it. Thinking back, it feels powerful – he was in his home city, playing at Soul:ution, his creation. And that was his last gig.

Marcus said to me, 'Be yourself, do your own thing, don't worry what anyone else is doing.' It stuck with me, and then when he passed it became stronger. He taught me to fuck all the bullshit off and get into this because of the art, to lose yourself in it. That's a big inspiration I've taken from the man, and it's shaped my musical path.”

It wasn't long before social platforms were pinging with heartfelt posts and comments from the music world and fans. In the long-read published by *Time Out** days after Marcus passed, the love and respect was palpable, and they still ring true.

*Written by Mark OD.

ZERO T

“He changed the direction of the whole music and was a figurehead for many artists coming through at that time.

When Marcus drew for your tune, you knew you were onto a winner! It's hard to accept I'll never have that unique pleasure again, but the legacy of the man and his music will inspire forever.”

STRATEGY

Biggest compliment I could pay Marcus is that he was genuine. Genuine guy, genuine music, genuine intentions. Everything that people love about the north-west was in him.

I went into his studio yesterday, as it seemed like the perfect place to take a moment to pay my respects, and as sad as it was, I felt so proud for him... the effect he has had on people worldwide is obvious and he did it all with zero compromising and kept it classy as fuck. One of my proudest moments in music was seeing my name next to the Soul:r logo on vinyl. It meant I'd fuckin' done something with my life. We are all his legacy.

My favourite Marcus quote? Being interviewed in Manchester one night, straight after the set, the interviewer asked him, 'What was it like playing back-to-back with Goldie?' Without any hesitation Marcus looked at him and said, 'Easy'.

GOLDIE

His thing for me was the humbleness of his music. He was so humble. Marcus really didn't give a fuck. He had no fear. There were tunes he wouldn't like, he would just say, 'I don't like it, it's a load of shite.'

There are people, like myself, who will make conceptual tunes for the rest of our lives. People like Calibre and Marcus. They make tune after tune after tune because they're seasoned. They've got massive consistency with huge dynamic. To me, Marcus is as impactful in this music (D&B) as J Dilla is to hip-hop.

Shortly after Marcus had passed, DRS and LSB put out a track to honour their mate, 'Angels Fall', with all proceeds going to Marcus's family. DRS somehow found the inner strength to lay down the pain he was feeling over LSB's production:

I text my dead friends' phones and I pray they'll answer
Just to hear their voice or engage in banter
To arrange one more night on the town
Remember when your absence is breaking me down
On the inside I'm screaming, outside faking a clown
Smiling hurts more when alone in the crowd
Staying silent when I wake in a sound
Is even more deafening when you're here in the clouds

I wish I never took that call
I wish I never knew at all
That angels fall

Tribute shows and features flooded the internet, each one containing personal anecdotes, funny memories, and celebrating Marcus's music. In a *UKF* article, Hospital Records founder Tony Colman, aka London Elektricity, recalled the support he'd received from Marcus in the label's early years.

TONY COLMAN LONDON ELEKTRICITY

"Marcus was pretty much the first person to welcome me and Chris Goss into D&B.

It was at the (*Knowledge* magazine) awards in 1999 in Kilburn and he was the smiliest, happiest, most positive person in a massive room full of D&B heads, nearly all of whom felt they had to look really moody and scowl at each other. Cos that was cool back then. But Marcus didn't give a shit about looking cool. And I loved him for that."

At the request of MC GQ, Fabio brilliantly corralled an impromptu four-hour Rinse FM show on 7 June with a who's who of the scene turning up for an emotional celebration which got progressively rowdier as it went on. For a scene that had lost the communal get-togethers of the Music House days, it was a reminder of the power drum & bass had to bring people together.

DJ Randall had all the heads in the studio in stitches with a story about being mistaken for Carl Cox by a guy at SunAndBass. Marcus mischievously got Jubei and others to start calling him Carl for the rest of the trip. DJ Storm affectionately saluted his refusal to compromise before saying, 'He was the grumpiest person I ever loved.' SP MC talked about the incredible depth of his back catalogue. Saul from Chase & Status, a duo who spent their early years making beats in Manchester, and Shy FX dropped in unannounced to pay their respects. There were belly laughs and teary moments aplenty, with the love for Marcus and his music audible in every syllable.

DOC SCOTT

"The show at Rinse FM was special. It made the scene come together. I remember that week after he left us, I've never seen the drum & bass scene that united.

It rocked everybody's soul so hard. I know for a fact that some people had problems with each other, and it got squashed, because people started to feel so united.

If something bad happens, you hope something good can come from it. And from Marcus passing, everyone came together like never before. That holds true to today. I like to think that's one of Marcus's lasting legacies."

As friends and family struggled to make sense of what had happened, Soul:ution had three events – in Manchester, London and Birmingham – under the banner '4Marcus'. Al Baker, Soul:ution's resident photographer, was there to capture the night at Manchester's Band on the Wall on 6 July.

AL BAKER

"I initially turned it down because, you know, you photograph a wedding, you don't photograph a funeral.

They told me to come, and I should take my camera, as I was an integral part of the night, and if I wasn't gonna photograph it, no one was. So in the end I took my camera and I'm really glad I did. I thought it would be a weird atmosphere, but it wasn't. It was very celebratory.

As the night went on and people got a bit drunk, there were loads of hugs and tears. I got lots of pictures of people laughing and crying, all in the same picture. Later on, they got his mum, Pat, out and introduced her to everyone. There wasn't a dry eye in the house. She spoke on the microphone about how she was aware of what Marcus did with DJing, but she'd never been interested. 'This is my first Soul:ution night,' she said, and the atmosphere was amazing. The whole room was applauding her and cheering. The last hour of photography was really difficult – I was crying, people I was photographing were crying. I've never been to anything like that. The energy and vibe in the room was massive."

For Pat, the experience of being present in Marcus's music world was brand new. The drum & bass community welcomed her with open arms, accepting her as one of their own. She had no idea of the journey she was about to embark on and the people she would meet.

After Marcus passed away, Soul:r went into probate. Six months later, Pat became the new director. 'I couldn't walk away from it, because there was nobody else to do it.' Over time, she familiarised herself with not just the business, but the processes that were involved, from production to accounts. Ayumi had been working on some admin aspects of the business, so Pat brought her on board as co–director, and together they have kept Soul:r alive in the spirit of Marcus, with help from Samurai Music's Geoff Wright.

AYUMI MAXWELL

> **"We felt very strongly that Marcus would not have wanted the label to go on without him, so with that in mind, our purpose became to protect and preserve his legacy, so that it would remain untouched as a true representation of his life's work."**

In a May 2018 *Mixmag* piece,* marking his one–year anniversary, many of his closest allies were clearly contemplating their own place in the world. The feeling of invincibility that comes with the flush of youth had been replaced by the sharp pain of mortality.

*Written by Mark OD.

DRS

> **"Death makes you re–evaluate where you sit in the world and what message you're going to leave as a musician or artist… I processed the grief of losing Marcus through my music."**

CALIBRE

“I loved Marcus like a brother, and like brothers, we had our differences, but one thing we always agreed on was music.

It wasn't just the soulful sounds, it was the way Marcus was an intelligent, relentless, perceptive, passionate and influential music man who loved a laugh and a moan.”

ZED BIAS

“I think Marcus's legacy runs a lot deeper than just his music catalogue. Musical relationships. Alliances. Friendships. He was a bloody genius, and a gentleman, and a very funny guy, especially when he wasn't trying to be funny, and he was just being grumpy!

He was a facilitator for Manchester music from day one. His music, and his record label Soul:r, transcended musical and geographical borders, and helped artists like DRS, Fox, Chimpo, Skittles, Dub Phizix, Strategy and Tyler Daley, to name a few. Now these guys are the dons, and they are leading the new lot through.”

Later that year, the blood, sweat and tears that those on the frontlines of Manchester's music scene had been putting in over many years was paying off. An army of artists, DJs and producers were bubbling up alongside frontrunners Children of Zeus and LEVELZ – a 14-strong collective featuring many of the names in this story (Dub Phizix, Chimpo, Fox and more). Zeus's debut album *Travel Light* became an instant classic in a city that's had its fair share of them. Dub Phizix, who was now regarded as one of the scene's leading producers, was clear on Marcus's role in a *Mixmag* Manchester feature.

DUB PHIZIX

“Marcus was the catalyst for everything we're seeing now. He created a culture of support in the city where helping people became the natural thing to do. Now that's been the state (of things) for a few years, we're starting to reap the rewards.”

SOUL:UTION CLASSICS

SELECTED BY JIM BANE

01. Marcus Intalex & ST Files – *How You Make Me Feel*
02. Calibre feat. Singing Fats – *Drop It Down*
03. M.I.S.T. – *Lose Control*
04. M.I.S.T. & High Contrast – *3AM*
05. Badmarsh & Shri – *Signs (Calibre Remix)*
06. M.I.S.T. v DJ Marky v XRS – *Back to Love*
07. Marcus Intalex – *Temperance*
08. Marcus Intalex – *Wide Eyes*
09. Commix – *Be True*
10. Breakage – *Clarendon*
11. Instra:mental – *Pacific Heights*
12. Alix Perez – *Crooklyn*
13. TEED – *Garden (Calibre Remix)*
14. Dub Phizix & Strategy – *The Editor*
15. Marcus Intalex & S.P.Y – *Celestial Navigation*
16. Dub Phizix & Fox – *Never Been*
17. DRS – *Bun Ya*
18. Dillinja – *I Wanna Know*
19. DRS feat. LSB & Tyler Daley – *The View*
20. DRS feat. Marcus Intalex – *Emergency*
21. Spirit – *International*

MARCUS FOREVER

Marcus left an unfillable void. Listen to DRS's 'Irreplaceable', written in the wake of losing his friend and mentor, and you'll hear just how deep it cut. It's no wonder DJ/producer Zero T has called Del 'the poet laureate of drum & bass'.

To honour Marcus, his legacy has been lovingly maintained by his closest family and friends, and the Marcus Intalex Music Foundation – a platform set up by his longtime friend Nick Sinna to 'nurture and guide musical talent'.

NICK SINNA

> **"The way that Marcus had supported people over the years, bringing people to the front, people who needed someone to give them that confidence, it felt like the right thing to do. Speaking to DRS and Pat about it, they agreed as well."**

Their events have given people the chance to come together and celebrate Marcus's life and music. The combination of education and workshops for young people from industry heavyweights, followed by an intense and sweaty club night, serves as a fitting tribute to a guiding light who helped so many up-and-coming artists follow their dreams.

In May 2018, Dub Phizix hosted a production masterclass to a room full of eager students as Martyn and Jenna G watched on. The late irrepressible DJ Randall turned up to show his support, taking the time to sit down with Pat Kaye for a coffee and a chat.

Later that night in the hot and sticky Soup Kitchen basement, the same venue Marcus had played his last set, DJs Special Request, DJ Lee and more tore the roof off as MC Fox shouted out the heads in the crowd and kept dancers moving with his mesmerising singjaying. It was one of those nights you leave feeling hot and giddy, full of a bittersweet happiness at what you've witnessed. It was a reminder of Marcus's timeless ability to stir the soul; the synth pads and bassline from 'Cabin Fever' haunted you for weeks on end afterwards.

Such is the respect for Marcus from all corners of the electronic music world, the Foundation has also been able to put on events featuring Marky, Goldie, Floating Points and Afrodeutsche. 'Floating Points used to buy drum & bass from Marcus at Eastern Bloc. He's got massive respect for him,' Nick explained. 'Youth services and funding have suffered since Covid. We'd love to do more but we've had to be a bit more sporadic. It's all self-funded, although Ableton did help us out for a while.'

This has seen Foundation events relocate from Manchester city centre to the Golden Lion in the West Yorkshire market town of Todmorden. Burnley is not far down the road, and Marcus's grandparents were originally from the town.

NICK SINNA

“We thought, we can do this in Manchester city centre, but being near Marcus's home in Burnley, we can engage with people in that area. We've had Goldie play, and MC workshops with Strategy. It's a pub with a great sound system. I can imagine it's the sort of place that if Marcus was around he'd say, 'That's fucking wicked.'”

Despite shrinking music track lengths, attention spans, and social media's insatiable demand for content, Marcus's anti-trends ethos still runs deep in the most innovative and credible D&B. It's like D&B's version of *Star Wars'* Resistance. Goldie, High Contrast and many more still have him in their thoughts when critiquing music, 'What would Marcus say?' Or 'Use the Force,' they hear… Only one of those is true. Labels like Dan Blindside and DRS's Space Cadet, Lenzman's The North Quarter and LSB's Footnotes are part of the lineage, but are critically doing their own thing.

One thing is for sure: Marcus would want all of his friends, family and industry allies to keep pushing things forward rather than dwell on the past. Marcus's close friend Doc Scott once said, 'I'm more interested in tomorrow than yesterday.' That was – and is – the mind-set that's kept underground drum & bass at the bleeding-edge of the electronic music scene over three decades and counting.

GOLDIE

"Marcus is always in my thoughts. Always. He's in my home in Thailand. Pat gave me his hat. It sits in my studio on top of my synths – an old Korg M1.

Above the hat is his picture. There's always a little twat lying around with his glasses saying, 'Ahhh, I dunno ya know.' He just had this great way of giving the nod to a tune that he'd love.

Marcus was very much the antichrist to commercial music, in a beautiful way. I sent him the vocals of 'Inner City Life' for him to have a crack at remixing, and forgot all about it. He just phoned me up one day and said, 'I've done this version, I'll send it to you before I mix it. See what you think, I don't really like it, though.' It was a very normal thing for Marcus not to like his own music. But he's a very powerful producer – no one will ever sound like him or be like him."

DOC SCOTT

I have a folder that I created on my record box called 'Not Marcus'. Any track I hear that I'm like, 'That sounds like Marcus,' it goes in.

More often than not, if you ask the artist they'll say they were thinking of Marcus when they made it. The music he made was so unique and distinctive, so when he left us there was this big, gaping hole. 'Not Marcus' probably has about 40-50 tracks in it. It just goes to show the power of his influence when he was alive and now when he's no longer around. He lives forever.

HIGH CONTRAST

I played him a tune I'd made for my second album called 'The Persistence of Memory'. When I saw him, he was like, 'You've done it. That is as good as it gets.'

It's not one of my big tracks, or one anyone's really mentioned to me, but Marcus singled it out. And it was a track that was influenced by Marcus and Lee's 'Neptune'. It has that sort of long journey, Detroit-type sound. When he said that, you can't beat that feeling.

We sometimes had our own differences. I was looking for more accessible sounds. Not consciously, but I was taking ideas from anywhere – the pop world or the underground world. I'd always have the voice of Marcus in my head, like an angel and devil. 'What would Marcus think of this tune?' still goes through my head.

CALIBRE

There's very few people who transcended the genre in the drum & bass world, but Marcus did. Marcus did something unique – perhaps it's underrated.

I still try to play one of his tracks almost every set. Some of the gigs I've done, I felt like Marcus was standing next to me. It's like a fleeting moment of feeling he's there.

ST FILES

Weirdly, he'd asked me to go round a year before he passed, and we started to make a tune. It'd been years since we'd done that.

We had a really good time. The tune's not the best, but we enjoyed messing about with a few samples. It reminded me of when we'd first started.

Ayumi said to me, 'Why don't you finish the track?' I said, 'If I could finish it, I would!' I asked out of curiosity if she knew what Marcus thought of the track. She said, 'Yeah, he said it was shit.'

TUNDE 2D BABALOLA (FUTURE CUT)

Anyone who has come through in the last 25 years or so owes him a debt of gratitude.

Manchester was renowned for northern soul, the Haçienda, techno, those early electro parties in Moss Side in the 80s. There's this mix of soulful sounds with industrial – that's what Marcus was able to incorporate into drum & bass.

DJ SAPPO

If Marcus was here, he'd be doing the same thing. He didn't follow trends or patterns. Always be a shepherd not a sheep, and he was definitely a shepherd.

DRS

I've been sober for over three years now. I remember saying to Pat, it was the grief from Marcus and Salford John (a much-loved D&B head on the Manchester scene) passing away (that made me) destroy myself.

I'm a writer, I'm inward, and I think about things a lot. In hindsight, I realise it's grief, and we use it as an excuse to destroy your life. It got to a point where I thought I'm actually gonna go down with this, or turn it around and turn it to light. I look at life like a learning process. Marcus was an anchor. He was a connector, and it's only after he's gone you realise the extent of that.

GEOFF WRIGHT (SAMURAI)

The whole magic of Marcus was how he crafted Soul:r. That's why it ceased to exist when he left us – who's gonna sign artists?

I'm helping them repress the catalogue, digital remasters and stuff like that. It's such a huge catalogue, and there's so much interest out there, too.

DJ FLIGHT

I feel like there's a gaping hole in my sets since Marcus passed. Soul:r was big, but underground big.

It didn't need to be any bigger – it wouldn't have been representative of what Marcus and Lee were trying to do.

Inevitably, for a label that reduced the number of records for each release to a few hundred copies during the streaming years, some of the prices on Discogs for original copies have hit crazy levels. Represses of 'The View Remix', *21* and Chimpo's 'Frontline'/'Buzzin' have been timely reminders of the gold in the Soul:r archives.

Fans have also been able to get their hands on releases Marcus had worked on with Jubei and the sadly missed Spirit, via Metalheadz, and SunAndBass Recordings. And there's been fresh Trevino music to enjoy.

Roberto, who went from partying on the Soul:ution dancefloor to becoming a widely-respected name in techno, put out his Trevino collaboration 'Formarcus EP', with all proceeds going to the Foundation. Roberto has since gone onto release on Metalheadz's techno imprint HeadzState – a pairing that Marcus would most certainly approve of.

Pat also made the decision to posthumously release a Trevino album. *Back* came out on Birdie in 2023. It was the successor to *Front*, released seven years earlier. Both artworks take inspiration from one of Marcus's favourite courses – Hillside in Southport.

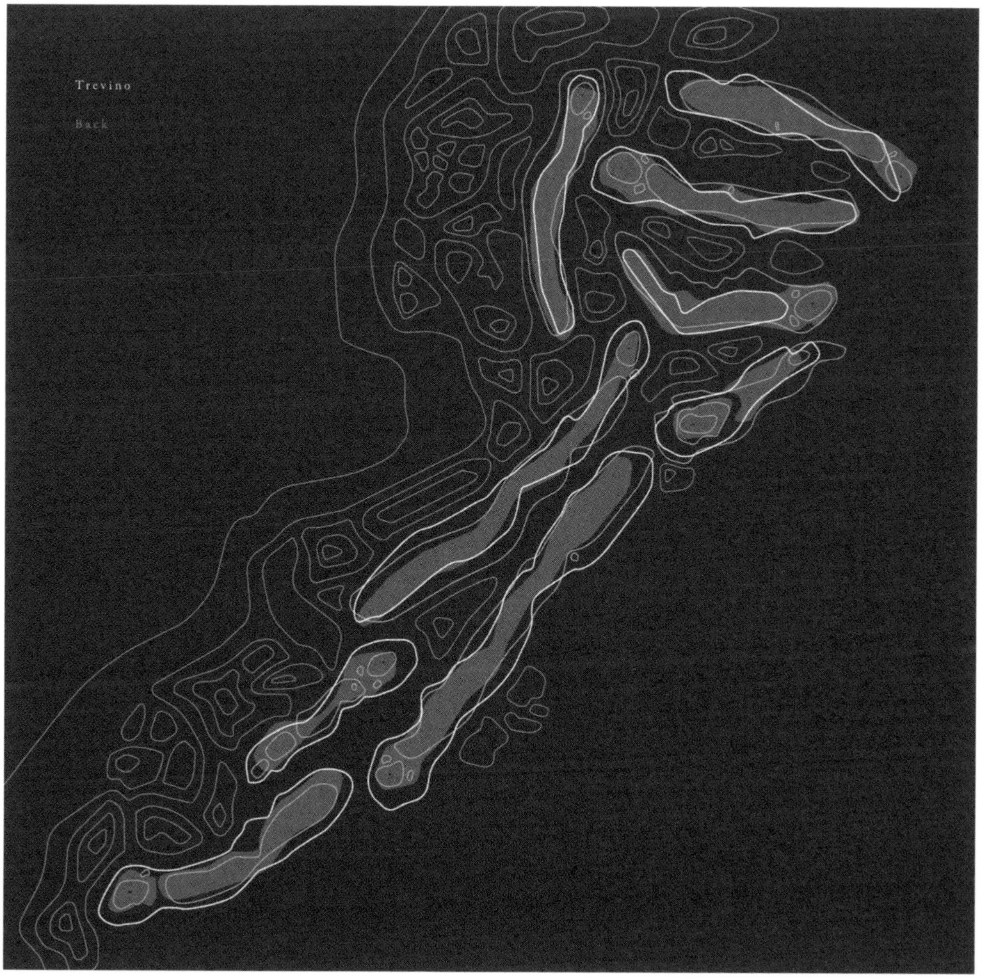

Trevino
Back

GOLDIE

“**Pat’s sharp and dry, and she can level you with her raw honesty. When I met her I thought, ‘Ah that’s where he gets it from.’**

She’s definitely Burnley personified. I’ve taken her flowers and sat down and had a Swiss roll. At her old place, I even pottered into the kitchen and washed up for her when she was upstairs. To have a sense of normality from the world that I come from is where we have an understanding.”

Many artists Marcus had championed and mentored found themselves grappling with how to move forward. The production duo Spectrasoul ended up releasing music that Marcus had personally signed off on before his death, as a way to pay their respects.

DAVE SPECTRASOUL

Marcus was an early adopter of our music. He championed us within his DJ sets and that was always an honour, but to then find out he wanted to sign an EP to his label Soul:r was the icing on the cake.

He signed off on the fourth and final track for the EP a few days before his untimely passing.

We didn't think about the music for a long time after, but had a few conversations with his nearest and dearest, who said that he would want the music to be out in the world for everyone to hear. So we released the EP on our Ish Chat label, with the running order exactly as Marcus had signed it. We also added a small tribute etching to the vinyl which shows up when you shine a bright light on it. Much like Marcus always was, shining bright.

HOBZEE SILENT DUST

Marcus is responsible for us becoming Silent Dust. It was actually the album name, which it still is, but we were Hobzee and Zyon Base. Marcus said, 'They're not good names. You sound like online IDs for World of Warcraft.'

Unfortunately, the album didn't come out on Soul:r. Off the back of that Marcus could have cut ties with us but instead he offered us a lot of support. The 14 tracks were done with the guidance of Marcus and Lee. He brought us together with DRS so we could collaborate with him, he remixed a tune, got Calibre to remix one, and got Om Unit to remix another. We decided to start our own label none60 Records, instead of going for a subpar label, and he gave us the support we needed. They always say, 'Don't meet your idol.' But it wasn't like that with Marcus. He didn't have an ego. He was a great guy and is thoroughly missed.

DJ MARKY

I'm a very passionate and a very sensitive person. He was very straight, sometimes rude, and grumpy, but I loved him!

We had a lot of fun together. He opened my eyes to a lot of things. The moments we shared were fantastic. I miss him every day. He's the only person that I have a photo of in my house.

ANDY C

He was a person who knew how to make tunes with maturity. They were expertly crafted, Marcus was absolutely unbelievable at that.

It's a legacy of thoughtful productions. He was a connoisseur and you can hear that in the music he made.

We owe it to the memory of people like Marcus to keep these tunes alive, and they will be kept alive. They'll be played forever. They're part of the heritage, part of the foundation of the scene.

TASHA

Neighbourhood is going to be 15 years old next year. We've built a community, and I couldn't be happier.

Marcus is one of the reasons why that is happening. I like to think I carry his spirit. He had such a big impact on my life and helped me believe in myself.

Beyond the music, there was a man from humble beginnings who stayed grounded and never let the acclaim go to this head. Back in Burnley, That 0282 Podcast had a fitting tribute shortly after he passed away.

It goes without saying how much the 0282 mailbag has been absolutely monopolised this past couple of weeks with folks sharing their thoughts and memories regarding the tragically premature passing of the top local boy – Marcus Intalex to many, Trevino to some, and to most who have messaged us, Marcus Kaye, whose voice opened this show followed by his track 'TB or not TB' off the *21* LP. Perhaps the only track I know that refers to both Roland (TB-303 synth) and Shakespeare. So fair play to you, Marcus.

The older Burnley heads, myself included, wax lyrical of the times down at Angels as kids, with Marcus on the decks making our nights again and again. In addition to the seemingly endless testimonies about his musical prowess, anyone who knew him will tell you how sound and clued up and how funny he was.

Marcus Kaye never strayed far from his roots. The singular vision, dedication to the artform and rejection of the trappings of mass appeal, can all be traced back to his formative years in his hometown. Even as his reputation as Marcus Intalex and Trevino soared, he remained grounded – the straight-talking, quick-witted, down-to-earth character who would remind friends to 'keep it chips 'n' gravy'. While his music back catalogue, Soul:r label, and role as a DJ and connector puts him up there with the greatest to ever do it, a piece of him never left Burnley.

LAST

BY PAT KAYE

The last time I saw Marcus was the day after his hole-in-one. We were supposed to be going for a meal.

He rang to tell me his great news and apologised for not being up to going out, but said he would bring some food.

He and Ayumi duly arrived – it's Marcus time! 'Get the kettle on Mum, I have brought a pork pie and a cheesecake for us to share, and Ayumi will have the cake.' The kettle went on, I cut the small pie, the cheesecake no bigger, in two and gave him a plate. He said he was cold and tired. Could I put the heating on, which I did, even though it was a warm day in May. Little did we know his time was running out! The food we ate whilst Marcus was telling about his hole-in-one, he was a proud and happy man. His ball, the cap and glove are now in a frame to remind me of his happy time.

Just before leaving he asked, 'Are the flowers on the mantelpiece lilies?' 'No,' I said. 'They are orchids.'

'I like them,' he replied and then off he and Ayumi went saying sorry again, and they would be over in two weeks to go for a meal.

When Marcus passed everyone who brought flowers had bought orchids or lilies – how strange is that! And of course they graced his coffin.

Music always lifts your spirits and takes you to a better place. Marcus was a master of that. We owe him a lot.

IMAGE CAPTIONS & CREDITS

Front Cover Marcus Intalex in 2011, taken by Ashes57, who he named the track 'From the Ashes' after on *21*. (Ashes57)

8 Taken from @marcusintalex on Instagram, posted on 5 May 2017. (Instagram)

10 Towneley High School football team in Belgium, 1984. Marcus on the far right stood up. (Kaye family)

16 'Jack Your Body' by Steve 'Silk' Hurley (1986). (DJ International Records)

19 Smackwater Jack's logo. (Smackwater Jack's)

21 Flyer for Gilly's night at the Bank Hall Miners, Burnley, 1987. (Gilly)

22 'Gilly and Marcus with Celebrity DJs' at Tony's Ballroom, 1988. (Gilly)

24-25 Flyer for Tony's Ballroom, c.1988-89. (Gilly)

26 Hysteria at Crackers, c.1988-89. (Neil Jackson)

27 (Top) Euphoria, Part 1, at the Kestrel Suite, Burnley, c.1988-89. (Gilly)

27 (Bottom) Chill-out at the Hop, Burnley, c.1988-89. (Gilly)

28-29 '300 held in Acid Swoop' – from the *Lancashire Evening Telegraph*, 26 November 1990. *(Lancashire Evening Telegraph)*

31 Marcus and Jason 'Jack' Frost at Churchill's, Accrington, c.1990-1991. (Gilly)

33 Marcus and Gilly (right) with two DJs who invited them to Dallas, USA, in the early 1990s. (Gilly)

34 'Keep Out!' Headline in the *Burnley Citizen*, 2 November 1989. *(Burnley Citizen)*

35 Power House – flyer from Monroe's, Great Harwood. (Neil Jackson)

37 Marcus and Gilly in Dallas, USA. (Gilly)

41 Marcus at the afters. (Gilly)

42 Flyer from the Kestrel Suite, Burnley, c.1989. (Gilly)

43 (Top) Flyer from Intense at Monroe's c.1989-90. (Neil Jackson)

43 (Bottom) Euphoria, Part 2, at the Kestrel Suit, Burnley, c.1988-89. (Gilly)

44-45 'Aftermath of an Acid House Party', 13 February 1990, originally featured in the *Burnley Express*. (Burnley Civic Trust Heritage Image Collection)

48 Marcus DJing at Angels, Burnley. c.1990. (Gilly)

49 Marcus and MC Ark at Angels. (Gilly)

52-53 Marcus and Paul Taylor at Angels. (Gilly)

56-57 Flyers from Vision at Angels, 1991-92. (Bodie Cameron)

59 Marcus and friends having a drink in the early 1990s. (Paul Hornsby)

62 Back of a flyer from Konspiracy nightclub, Manchester. (MDMArchive)

67 Flyer from Vision at Angels. (Bodie Cameron)

68-69 Marcus and Graham 'Grumpy' Naylor in Ibiza, 1994. (Paul Hornsby)

72 Cover of *Atmosphere* magazine, issue 26, 1995. (Paul Reson)

75 'Something For Your Mind'. From the fanzine *Gunslingers* from the mid-90s. (Rachel Newsome)

77 Mark XTC and Marcus. (Mark XTC)

79 (Top) Da Intalex – 'What Ya Gonna Do' / 'Nice & Slow' (Flex Records, 1994). (Mark OD)

79 (Bottom) Pictures of Marcus and Mark XTC in action. (Mark XTC)

80 & 82 Intalex Productions record and sleeve. (Paul Reson)

86-87 Clipping from *Muzik* magazine from the mid-90s. *(Muzik)*

88 Guidance at Music Box flyer, 1998. (Sherif Dhaimish)

92 Future Cut & M.I.S.T. in the studio. (Future Cut)

93 (Top left) Marcus DJing, Calibre in the background. (Future Cut)

93 (Top right) Marcus in the mix. (Future Cut)

93 (Bottom) Marcus, agent Kevin Gimble and Future Cut. (Future Cut)

94-95 'How You Make Me Feel' / 'Neptune' by Marcus Intalex & ST Files, 2000. (31 Records)

96-97 M.I.S.T., early 2000s. (Cleveland Aaron)

98-99 4hero – 'Les Fleur' / '9x9' Remixes, 2001. (Talkin' Loud)

97 M.I.S.T. featured in *Knowledge* magazine, November 2002. *(Knowledge)*

103 Soul:r record box artwork from the archive. (Soul:r)

104-05 & 107 Selection of Soul:r early records. (Soul:r)

110-111 Crowd shot from Soul:ution/1Xtra night at Band on the Wall, 14 November 2003. Special Guest DJ Zinc. (Al Baker)

112 2004 flyer from Soul:ution. (Gawain Forster)

114-115 Marcus had just handed DJ Marky the white label promo of Calibre's 'Mr Maverick' / 'Highlander'. Soul:ution at Band on the Wall, Manchester, 13 February 2004. (Al Baker)

117 DRS crowdsurfing at the launch party for his album *I Don't Usually Like MCs, But...* (Soul:r, 2012) at Soul:ution, Band on the Wall, Manchester, 26 August 2012. (Al Baker)

121 DJ Flight and Marcus at Soul:ution, Band on the Wall, Manchester, 21 March 2003. (Al Baker)

122-123 *DAT:Music* artwork from 2006. (Soul:r)

124 Calibre, ST Files and Marcus having a pint at Jackson's Boat, Sale. Featured on the cover of *Knowledge*, January 2007. (Cleveland Aaron)

126 Press release for Mist:i:cal's album *The Eleventh Hour*, 2007. (Soul:r)

127 Mist:i:cal's *The Eleventh Hour* LP cover, released in 2007. (Soul:r)

130 Calibre at Soul:ution, Band on the Wall, Manchester, 19 March 2004. (Al Baker)

133, 135 & 152 Marcus at the Grove Golf Club, Hertfordshire, for an Atmosphere photoshoot, March 2009. (Cleveland Aaron)

136 'Astro Dance EP' by Marcus Intalex, 2008. (Soul:r)

138 Broke 'n' English's 'Nothing Will Come Of It' EP, 2003. (Estate Recordings)

141 Cover art of Marcus Intalex's LP *21*. Released in 2011. (Soul:r)

142-43 Marcus in his studio, Manchester. (Chelone Wolf)

146-47 Marcus in the studio with Lynx, and DRS in Manchester. (Chelone Wolf)

154 Ayumi and Marcus in the booth. (Ayumi Maxwell)

155 Marcus Intalex in the mix. (Thumbs Footage)

158 Trevino's *Front* LP cover art. Released in 2016 on Birdie. The artwork for this and *Back* (2023) was inspired by Marcus's favourite course – Hillside, Southport. (Soul:r)

159 'Four Fit EP' by Marcus Intalex. Released in 2016. (Soul:r)

160-161 Marcus up close. (Chelone Wolf)

170 Crowd shot from the emotional memorial night, 4Marcus at Band on the Wall, Manchester. 6 July 2017. (Al Baker)

171 DJ Marky playing at the 4Marcus night, with Ayumi and Dan Blindside behind him. (Al Baker)

179 The cover of Trevino's *Back* LP, released on Birdie posthumously in 2023. (Soul:r)

180 Goldie headlining the Marcus Intalex Music Foundation's night at the Golden Lion, Todmorden. 27 February 2022. (Paul Reson)

185 Marcus in the studio, Manchester. The photo was used to inspire the cover of Jubei & Marcus Intalex's 'Lubbly Jubbly / Fanny's Your Aunt', released posthumously on Metalheadz in 2018. (Jubei)

WRITERS

Sherif Dhaimish is a publisher, writer, and champion of local stories. As director of Pendle Press, Sherif spotlights narratives primarily from his native Burnley, Lancashire – including Marcus Kaye's remarkable life and music. His recent collaborations include publishers like Manchester University Press and New Dimension, producing an eclectic range of books. With degrees from the University of Leeds and King's College London, Sherif's writing has appeared in *Left Cultures*, *New Lines*, and *nb. Magazine*. He bridges local heritage with global perspectives, bringing engaging stories to light.

Follow him at @sherif_dhaimish

Mark O'Donnell, aka Mark OD, originally championed the Manchester drum & bass scene during its rise to global prominence in the late 90s and 00s. As a DJ, co-founder of the Metropolis club night and writer, Mark reported from the frontlines of the scene and documented key players (Marcus Intalex & ST Files, Sonic & Silver, Sappo, Jenna G, Broke 'n' English and more) through seminal print publications *Knowledge* and *Atmosphere* magazine, subsequently becoming editor of *Atmosphere* and putting Marcus on a golf-themed cover in 2009. He's subsequently written for *Mixmag*, *Time Out* and *Bandcamp Daily*, and believes Marcus's music, both solo and collabs, put him up there with the greatest to ever do it.

Follow him at @markodonnell23

DESIGNER

Luke Pajak is a multi-discipline artist specialising in the arts, music, television and not-for-profit industries, with a diverse clientbase including Oxfam, Kidscape, Pendle Press, Bonafide Films and Ringside Studios. His work involves a mixture of graphic design, photography and illustration and his education consists of a First Class degree in Photography & Design and a Masters in Photography from London College of Communication.

Follow him at @lukepajak

SHOUT OUTS

Al Baker
Andrew Campy
Antagonist
Ants Kolaitis
Ashes57
Ayumi Maxwell
Ben Ash
Blindside
Bodie Cameron
Calibre
Chelone Wolf
Children of Zeus
Chimpo
Chris Parkinson
Cleveland Aaron
Colin Steven
Darwin
Dave Spectrasoul
DJ Flight
DJ Marky
DJ Pale
DJ Sappo
Doc Scott
DRS
Dub Phizix
Eric Brünjes
Fox
Future Cut
Gawain Forster
Geoff Wright
Glenn AI
Goldie
Graham 'Grumpy' Naylor
High Contrast
Hobzee
Jason 'Jack' Frost
Jenna G
Jim Bane
Jubei
Levelz
Longman
LSB
Luke Pajak
Mark XTC
Martyn
Martyn Arkwright
Neil Jackson
Nick Sinna
Nigel 'Gilly' Gilmartin
Oliver Yorke
Pat Kaye
Paul Hornsby
Paul Reson
Paul Taylor
Rahul Verma
Randall
Rich Reason
Sonic & Silver
ST Files
Strategy
Tasha
That 0282 Place
Thumbs Footage
Tonn Piper
Wilf Prophecy
Zed Bias

How You Make Me Feel wouldn't have been possible without the generosity of the above people. A special thank you to Attack Magazine (2014), Resident Advisor (2016) and Red Bull Music Academy (2003) for permission to use transcripts from interviews with Marcus; also to Paul Reson for producing the book's trailer.

SHERIF DHAIMISH

Thank you to all who helped bring this story together through powerful words and images. Pat, special thanks for welcoming me into your home for countless brews and chats about Marcus and Burnley. To Sarah, habibti, for your love and support; and Luke, for the creative spark (and patience) that brought this project to life on the page.

MARK O'DONNELL

A massive big-up to the Manchester jungle/drum & bass scene for a lifetime of inspiration. To the scene's originators: I salute you. Much love to everyone who entrusted Sherif and I with their stories and memories. Shout out to Rahul Verma for helping us with copy edits. Thank you to Pat and Ayumi for their encouragement, feedback and blessing for the book. To the one and only Khads for all the love and support and that night with Marcus on the dancefloor at Pépé Bradock.

Big shout out to everyone who preordered *How You Make Me Feel.*

Ciaran Abel, Julian Adam, Dan Adams, Robert Adams, Luke Agacy, Jamie Agnew, Luke Argilla, Louis Alden, Lottie Aldridge, Alegria, Tsvetomir Soulnd Alekov, Casto Alonso, Ethan Anderson, Troy Anderson, Antagonist, Fróði Árnason, Leon Ashdown, Alan Attias, James Austin, Oliver Bagshaw, Rowan Bailey, Frederic Balduck, Marcus Barnes, Darren Barton-Taylor, Tom Bassi, Paul Beales, Matt Bean, Stuart Beattie, Sean Beeby, Matthew Belwood, Damian Bennett, Paul Bennett, Sebastian Bennett, Alex Bentley, Balazs Benyo, Christopher Bertenshaw, Saurabh Bhabuta, Michael Biber, John Biddle, Gabor Blaho, Michael Blandford, Mikey Blesid, Daan Boerrigter, Matt Bone, Connor Borrett, Mark Brennan, Chris Brentano, Grant Brothwell, Lee Brown, Toyacoyah Brown, Ed Brown-Jackson, Andre Buckles, Matthew Bush, Bardo Camp, Mauro Campana, John Cappo, Jennifer Carnegie, Will Case-Toussaint, CassDubWild, James Chambers, Johnnie Chan, John Chapman , Robert Chisnall, Dean Church, Adam Churchill, Owen Clarke, Nick Claydon, Lee Clinch, Myronn Codrington, Kirsty Colahar, Morgan Connolly, Sam Constable, Shawn Conte, Jane Costain, Darren Crawley, Dan Crowley, Jonathan Cumming, Scott Cunliffe, Michal Cvik, Tom Dagless, Nikki Darham, Greg Day, Ian De Smet, Kishan Deva-Aditya, Emmanuel Devezeaux, Shawn DeVries, Hanna Dhaimish, Will Dickie, Omma Soul:ution Disciple, Freddie Dixon, Harry Dockerty, Si Donnelly, Jake Drysdale, Ashley Dutton, Nigel Edmonds, Simon Ellacott, Jonathan Ellis, Christoph Eppensteiner, Ian Fernandez, Chris Few, Anthony Finch, Diligent Fingers, Finn Finneran, Paul Fletcher, Adrian Flynn, Tim Forrester, Gawain Forster, Alistair Fraser, Tom Gammons, John Garratt, Steven Gaughan, Michael Genato, Daljit Gill, Anthony Gillespie, Michael Gillies, Paul Gold, Alex Gould, Sadie Graham, Duncan Grant, Chris Green, Darragh Guilfoyle, Travis Guillaume, Alex Hagley, Sam Hailstone, Matthew Hamilton, Nung Hammad, Thomas Hamp, Lee Hammond, Guy Harwood, Andy Hatt-Cooney, Steven Haw, Clearwater Hawes, Simon Headlam, Kate E Heaps, Kieran Heaven, Steve Hegarty, Rick Hibbert, James Hillah, Jon Hillman, Ben Hindle, Martin Hodgson, Roger Hoggett, Andrew Holden, Alex Holt, Nick Hopkins, Adrian Hopson, David Horkay, Lucie Hugary, Chris Hughes, Andy Hunter, Gillian Ingham, James Ingles, James Irving, Martin Ivanov, Joel Jackson, Tom Jackson, Stephen Jacobs, Krea James, Jacob Jay, Andrew Jeffery, Jack Jennings, Chris Johnson, Gareth Jones, Mark Jones, Michael Jones, Paul Jones, Stephen Jones, Saul Jordaan, Tim Kantoch, DJ Kingsize (Dawn Raid), Max Kirk, Rob Kirkaldy, Anthony Kolaitis, Ursa Krivc Romih, Kristjan Kroupa, Dylan Lally, Henry Lake, Walter Jack Lanham, Andrew Lees, Patrick Leonard, Darren Lewis, Michael Lowney, Joe Lucas, Tom Maddex, Stuart Mair, Jesse Mann, Ashley Maroney, Filip Martens, Sophie Matera, Neil McCullough, Phil McFarland, Leo McGivney, Kevin McKernan, Joel McLagan, Finn Maclean, Daniel A Medina, Darren Mellor, Dean Merrick, Marius G. Mevold, Marc Miller, Matt Millin-Brawn, Jon Moakes, Oliver Moore, Craig Moorhouse, Rafa Morataya, Igor Moroz, David Moss, Brendon Mullins, Jon Murray, Olivia Mustain, Tariq Najam, Nikhil Nayee, Benjamin Ness, Richard Nestor, Chris Newbery, Andrew Nicholas, Jennifer Nicholls, Khadeen O'Donnell, Taur Ojala, Simon O'Leary, George Palmer, Matt Parkin, Oli Parris, Stephen Payne, Keiran Perry, Libby Petch-Stewart, James Phillips, Dustin Pituch, Tom Potten, Stephen Potvin, Nick Powney, Carlos Puga, Matt Price, Ryan Purcell, James Purchase, Robbie Radisa, Damien Ratcliffe, Alfred Reynolds, Ryan Reynolds, Alex Richards, Paul Rietveld, Bram Rijvers, Alyah Rivière, Jo Rogel, Jake Rogers, Vanity Roxane Lammers van Toorenburg, Brooke Russell, Robert Russell, Richard Sadler, Michael Salerno, Daniel Sanderson, Samuel Sayer, Michiel Schauwvliege, Giacomo Schiaffini, Eric Schirtzinger, Cameron Schmidt, Andrew Secrett, Alex Sheppard, Roger Shore, Magnus Skjåk-Bræk, Joseph Smaje, Dave Smith, Luke Smith, Quinn Smith, Shane Smith, Dan Soulsmith, Dave SpectraSoul, Rik Staesens, Shannon Stark, Andreas Stellatos, Marlon Sterling, Scott Strachan, Mark Swift, Kamil Sztuczka, Prijay Tailor, Peter Tanasovich, Tim Tetlow, Maria Thomas, Julia Tillmanns, Corwin Troje, Karl Tryggvason, Russell Turner, Nik von Frankenberg, Paul Van Massey, Dave Varol, Villem, Max Ward, Rob Warden, Kenji Watanabe, James P White, Paul White, Ross Whyman, Joshua Wild, Joe Wilkinson, Luke Wilson, David Winsett, Jake Witherington, DJ WOO, David Wright, Nick Wright, Dustin Zahn

First published in 2024 by Velocity Press

Produced by Pendle Press
PP008

velocitypress.uk
pendle-press.co.uk

Printed and bound in Poland by Interak

Design
Luke Pajak

Cover photo by Ashes57

ISBN: 9781913231675